Other Books by Margaret Halsey

WITH MALICE TOWARD SOME
SOME OF MY BEST FRIENDS ARE SOLDIERS

COLOR BLIND

A White Woman Looks at the Negro

by

MARGARET HALSEY

SIMON AND SCHUSTER
New York, 1946

For
Captain James Canfield Fisher
and
Lieutenant Robert K. Haas, Jr.

In Memoriam

TABLE OF CONTENTS

———

I

Color Conscience

———

THE SHREWD and speculative reader—of whom, I always think, I have more than my fair share—will perhaps wonder why I, of all people, should be writing this book. It is a book about race relations, a deadly serious subject, whereas my publishers cause it to be printed in places marked "(adv.)" that I am a humorous writer.

The answer is simple. Humorists are not humorous twenty-four hours a day. In fact, when you get to know them well, they are often not humorous at all. They tend to be hypersensitive, taut, neurotic creatures driven by God knows what obscure compulsion to earn their living the hard way.

The professional humorist catches cold, is jilted in love, pays income tax, and worries about the atomic bomb. If at any time he appears to be merry and relaxed about these phenomena, it is only because he has signed a contract with somebody involving the receipt of money. His family could tell you another story. And when, as happened to me, he finds himself in a situation which includes the Negro-white patterns of our country, he reacts as a citizen and not as a jester.

It is my reckless habit—and considering that I write them myself, you would think I would be more careful—to classify books as Greater Thises or Lesser Thats. But if I were reading this book, instead of writing it, I would not know in what category it belonged. Most writing on the race problem falls into one of two classes. Either it is passionate fiction about race clashes, lynchings, and various forms of violence and degradation or else it is passionless nonfiction, loaded to the gunwales with statistics about wages and graphs about venereal disease. This volume is neither. I have never seen a race clash, and I am not equipped to write a treatise. I worked for some years in a project which was, among other things, interracial. These pages have no justification beyond the fact that I was there, and this is how it seemed to me.

For the Negro-white relationships I have touched on in the following chapters, I had no especial background or preparation. There were no Negroes in the rather remote suburban neighborhood where I grew up, and none in the grammar school I attended. The only mammy I had was the white lady who had put herself to the inconvenience of bearing me, and as a child I never saw Negroes except in the streets and stores and public utilities. I do not remember being instructed in any particular way of thinking or feeling about them. As I recall it, nobody ever talked about them at all.

There may have been Negro students at the high school I went to, which was a large one in an industrial town, but I do not remember. At college I was first introduced to the social sciences and read in books about the chronic and systematized injustice with which our Negro citizens have to contend. This filled me with a sense of outrage, but the people around me persisted in being Caucasians and I could think of nothing specific and immediate to do. Perhaps I did not try very hard. I was preoccupied in those days with a series of line plungers and running backs whose personal life I aspired to be a feature of, and my subconscious conclusion may very well have been that I had done enough merely by being indignant, and that for the rest, the Negroes would have to wait.

When I was twenty-five, I got around to doing something about race relations. That, at least, was what I thought at the time. I took an apartment and employed a Negro maid. Her name was Jeannette, and she has been on my conscience ever since. Aside from the fact that she was middle-aged, I knew nothing at all about Jeannette qua Jeannette. To me, she was the entire Negro race, and I was going to make up to her for all the indignities which had been visited on her section of the populace over a period of several hundred years. Disastrous is no word for what this little project turned out to be. It would be hard to say who was the more bewildered, angry and confused—Jeannette or I—and in the end I was mercifully released from a completely untenable situation when Jeannette's doctor said she would have to get some kind of work which did not involve her being so much on her feet.

I have had subsequent Negro maids, but only in the pedestrian and unambitious way in which I employ a white maid—i.e., they cleaned my house and I paid them for it.

That was, until a while ago, the sum of my experience with our largest minority. It does not add up to much. Indeed, I would not mention that combination I had of innocence, ignorance, indifference and inexperience if it were not that a great many other well-meaning white Americans have it, too. And are troubled about it. I thought that they, in particular, might be interested in the reflections and conclusions hereinafter contained.

II

Color Conscious

———

I REMEMBER VERY distinctly the first time I ever entertained a Negro in my house. There was quite a background to it. I was just sitting there quietly spinning on my axis—clucking disapprovingly over shipments of scrap iron to Japan, but not writing any letters to Congress about it—when it turned out that a great many other people hadn't written any letters to Congress, either, and Pearl Harbor materialized. My husband disappeared into an organization which succeeded, where I failed, in making him pick things up, and I went to work at a servicemen's canteen.

I was at the Awkward Age for working in a canteen. I was thirty-one, almost thirty-two. At thirty-one, almost thirty-two, you are regarded by a canteen clientele which is mostly ten years your junior as too old to be interesting, but not quite withered enough to pinch-hit for Dear Old Mom. The canteen, therefore, astutely disposed of me and my contemporaries by making us captains of shifts of Junior Hostesses. We each had a group of young women ranging in age from, roughly, eighteen to twenty-five, and it was our responsibility to see that they were regular in their attendance and demure rather than provocative in their deportment.

The canteen where I went to work did not discriminate against Negroes. Negro servicemen were welcomed impartially along with the white boys, and of the fifty or sixty Junior Hostesses on my shift, about five or six were Negroes. These Negro Junior Hostesses were my first experience of Negroes in any role other than that of janitor or maid, and they were soothing. Mostly college girls, well bred and well dressed, they were no more of a responsibility than the white Junior Hostesses, except for one thing. There is a certain type of white man who feels that any Negro woman, no matter how stately her conduct, is a legitimate target for the crudest sort of sexual advances, and this manner of man does not dissuade easily. Some of my Negro Junior Hostesses occasionally had distasteful experiences of a

6

kind that no white girl who wears clothes when she goes out is called upon to handle.

Did I say my Negro Junior Hostesses were soothing? This is not entirely true. In the beginning, I was not soothed by them. Freedom from prejudice is one thing in theory and quite another in actual practice. Realistically speaking, it is impossible for white people who have been accustomed to Negroes only in menial roles to be entirely at ease when they first start meeting educated Negroes on a footing of equality. All the good will in the world will not keep one's eye from bouncing off the dark skin or one's mind from forming the breathless thought, "I'm talking to a Negro." To these sensations are added a miserable sense of guilt, for having such reactions at all, and a rather sickly hope that the confronting Negro will not divine them. The Caucasian is a startled and uncomfortable citizen the first time he discovers that equality is not automatic, but has to be learned.

I started out by referring to the first time I entertained a Negro in my house, but it is a singularly pointless story. Nothing happened. I met a Negro girl at a committee meeting and impulsively asked her to come home with me. She is a pretty girl, and of a most engaging color, but I was not entirely comfortable when I walked down the street with her. I wondered whether people were staring, and I

7

was afraid that some hot-eyed Confederate would leap out from behind a lamppost and start denouncing me—in which case I knew that my reply would not measure up to the Gettysburg Address.

However, we reached my house without disturbing the equilibrium of the East Forties, and had a glass of sherry and talked for a while. For the first few minutes, I had a feeling—none the less vivid although I knew it was irrational—that my guest would be in some way different from other guests, because she was a Negro. But she turned out to be absolutely identical with all my other visitors. She went like a homing pigeon to the chair with the broken springs, and out of a dozen little table ornaments, she picked up the particular one that is split down the middle and comes apart when you handle it. We talked about various things—things connected not with the race problem, but only with the none too voluptuous experience of being a human being. And then she left. That was all there was to it, except that as a venture into the brotherhood of man, it was much less taxing than listening to Fourth-of-July oratory or reading editorials in the papers.

I have gone on at great length about my own feelings when playing hostess to a Negro girl, but I have said nothing about her feelings. That is because I do not know what they were. Negroes do not tell white people how they feel, and if they did, it would not ring a bell with us. The Negro American has had a whole body of experience—ranging from snubs, either subtle or boorish, all the way up to lynching—which the white American has not had; and no white man can, with any accuracy, claim to know the Negro until the life patterns of the two groups are considerably closer than they are now. White people who say they "understand" the Negro merely mean that they have seen a lot of Negroes around; but this does not imply a mastery of their psychology any more than living next door to Einstein implies a mastery of the theory of relativity.

Equality is an unconscious assumption, and if you feel you are treating someone as an equal, then you are not doing it. This basic unconscious assumption has to be learned, and it has to be learned through personal experience. Until it is taught to them, white children have no prejudice against Negro children. But white adults, no matter how technically free from prejudice, cannot react to Negroes with childlike composure and stability unless they have a little practice. An enormous amount of legend and emotion adheres to the Negro American, and legend and emotion seep into the blood stream silently and without the owner's knowledge. I should not have said, for myself, that I believed all Negroes are lazy. But I must have believed it in part, because I was surprised when I discovered— through talking and writing to Negro servicemen, and working on committees with Negro civilians—

that some Negroes are as compulsively hard-working as the most repressed and anxiety-ridden New England housewife.

In moments of stress, people's principles sometimes collapse, but what a person has actually experienced becomes a part of him and never fails him. The war gave race relations an enormous push in the direction of either resolution or disaster. It is too soon yet to tell which. But at this point in man's upward struggle toward the stars, it is imperative to have as many white people as possible whose actual experience of Negroes as equals—not whose principles, but whose actual experience—enables them to take a realistic and nonlegendary view of colored Americans.

III

"Trouble"

THE CANTEEN where I worked could hold up its head with any similar oasis when it came to providing sandwiches and other divertissements; but the bright jewel in its crown was its policy of not discriminating against Negroes. This policy was in operation for four years, and it worked. It worked because the people who launched it and kept it going wanted it to work. These people, unable because of age and/or sex to die for the American ideal, decided to take second best and live with it.

The no-discrimination policy upon which, in this connection, they embarked had a twofold effect. Among Negroes who came in contact with it, it built up a little desperately needed good will toward the American Caucasians. (Our Negro compatriots— and it scarcely requires a slide rule to figure out why—take a very dim view of white people, *any* white people, and are not generally disposed to regard same as Queen of the May.) The other result of the no-discrimination policy was that it gave white people a chance to meet and talk to and work with Negroes who were not wearing bandannas or carrying mops. Although it was planned as an organization for entertainment, the canteen inadvertently became a sort of educational institution.

When the no-discrimination policy was first proposed, some of the canteen's supporters broke the world's record for the standing backward jump. To these startled people, the equalitarian contingent stressed the fact that in neighborhoods inhabited by high explosive, tan and brown and black men become just as dead as white ones.

"Yes, I know, BUT . . ." the Timid Souls replied, and went on to say that although they were wholeheartedly for the policy in theory, they were afraid that in actual practice it would only have the unhappy effect of embarrassing the Negroes. Their real fear, of course, was that the policy would embarrass, not the Negroes, but the Timid Souls themselves. However, the equalitarians pointed out that any Negro who is born in the United States and lives there till the age of twenty has already been so decisively embarrassed that one little bit more isn't going to make very much difference. Particularly if it occurs in connection with a sincere attempt to close the unseemly gap between our democratic protestations and our actual behavior.

The Timid Souls then resorted to the vague and murmurous affirmation which has swallowed up and blotted out so many nursling efforts to practice real democracy toward the Negro. There would be "trouble," the Timid Souls said. This word "trouble"—nervously invoked by individuals who bear the Negro no ill will, but who are very careful to what geese they say, "Boo!"—can probably hold its own with the Ku Klux Klan as an instrument for keeping the Negro American a second-class citizen. Nobody ever says specifically of what the "trouble" is going to consist. It is merely necessary to pronounce the word, and all the concepts of democracy, liberty, justice, fair play and implemented Christianity vanish like fluff in a hurricane.

The canteen's equalitarians refused to let themselves be stopped by the word "trouble." They pressed for a more definite answer. What kind of "trouble"? The first reply was—race riots. The equalitarians answered that, surprising as it may seem, men in the armed forces could not drop into canteens and recklessly start race riots, no matter how luscious and tempting the prospect might appear to them. It was a procedure that got them into trouble (no quotes) with their C.O.'s.

In the course of four years, the canteen entertained about three million, two hundred thousand servicemen, from all the United Nations. With so large and varied a pastorate, it was reasonable to expect that occasions might sometimes arise wherein one warrior would decide the hell with Socratic dialogue and take a poke at another warrior. For this contingency, provision was made. The orchestra was instructed, if a fight threatened, to play *The Star-Spangled Banner,* during which all servicemen have to stand at attention. This gave the canteen officials time to reach the scene and straighten things out.

The arrangement turned out to be almost unnecessary. In four years, there were only two such contretemps. Once a white Marine tried to pull a Negro sailor away from a white girl he was dancing with. And once an argument between a white Canadian sailor and a white American sailor about whether the United States was pulling its weight in the war degenerated into fisticuffs. In both cases the national-anthem technique worked perfectly and the disturbance was only momentary. On no occasion did the M.P.'s or the Shore Patrol have to be sent for in a hurry. For us, the "trouble" so often envisioned by those of little faith turned out to be purely imaginary.

We who worked at the canteen were often asked: What did Southern servicemen do, when they came into the canteen and found Negroes mingling with white people? The answer is that, for the most part, they didn't do anything. The proportion of people brought up to have moderately good manners is just as high in the South as it is in any other part of the country. Besides, there was nothing the South-erners *could* do. They were just as helpless as North-erners who visit the South and have to go around in an anguish of impotence reading "For White Only" signs.

Sometimes a Southerner for whom the emotional shock of the no-discrimination policy was more than he could bear would seek out a Junior or Sen-ior Hostess, or the person in charge of the canteen, and explain in vigorous language just what he thought of such goings-on. With tactful handling— which meant a sympathetic understanding of the blind panic behind the Southerner's raging and in-temperate language—these individuals could some-times be brought to concede that we had as much right to our idiosyncrasies as they had to theirs. (We had more, but it is not a point there is much percentage in ramming home all at once.) Almost uniformly, the Southerners were not angry with the Negroes for being there. They were angry with the white people who had invited them in. And, of course, the Southern serviceman always had one last

15

string to his bow. He could always flounce out in a huff.

As a matter of fact, the canteen's no-discrimination policy came, with the passage of time, to be accepted more and more unquestioningly. This may have been in part because it worked. In addition, as the months elapsed and white servicemen began returning from overseas—where they were caught up with Negroes in the leveling exigents of warfare—their complaints about having to share a canteen with the darker brother dwindled and began to die away. But perhaps the main reason why the policy ultimately came to be pretty much taken for granted was that it had behind it the whole spirit and intent of a couple of weatherbeaten documents called the Constitution and the Declaration of Independence. These antique publications, it is comforting to note, still have a good deal of prestige and influence. You have to be willing to trust yourself to them to find out how much.

But the word "trouble," brought forward as an excuse for continuing to deny simple justice to the Negro American, means more than race riots. After the issue of race riots is raised and met, the question is far from closed. On the contrary, we find that we're off in a cloud of lust. To that tindery and inflammable entity, the American imagination, the word "trouble" suggests a vision or fantasy of millions of beautiful white girls being seduced by

Negro men with the machinelike regularity of a sexual Willow Run. Whereupon each beautiful white girl produces—almost instantly, too—a coal-black baby with purple high lights. In the American imagination, when the word "trouble" is invoked, these coal-black babies patter down into the national scene like berries into a quart measure.

From a practical point of view, however, the production of coal-black babies by white women is not the lead-pipe cinch it is dreamed to be. In any work involving extensive contact with Negroes, one of the first things one notices is how few Negro Americans are coal-black. The clamorous insistence of some Southerners that the two races must never mingle is not without its diverting side. White men have been cohabiting with Negro women for several hundred years, and so extensive and effective has this mingling of the races been that the American Negro is referred to by scientists as a mulatto and not as a true Negro type at all, the West African Negro being considered the model of the pure Negro type. Every year, thousands of the Negro population of the United States "pass" and go to live with the white population, as whites—a migration in which they have been liberally assisted by the forefathers of some of the very people who are most adamant against a mingling of the races.

A white woman, therefore, wishing impishly to surprise the folks at home with a jet-hued grandchild, cannot just go out and lay her hands on a coal-black sire. Coal-black sires take a bit of finding. And once found, there is no guarantee that the resultant offspring will be coal-black. Generally speaking, the child of a white person and a Negro tends to be somewhat lighter in color than the Negro parent. That story which is the darling of so many strongly prejudiced people—the story about two apparently white people who produce a coal-black baby because one of the parents had Negro ancestry —is a myth.

On this point, science is inexorable. Those ebony "throwbacks" so dear to the hearts of the Rinso-whites are genetically impossible. The people who assure you that they know for a certainty that "throwbacks" are possible, because their husband's sister's cousin's friend had one, are admitting to more than they might perhaps wish to acknowledge. Two apparently white people produce apparently white babies, unless—and even this is a very remote possibility—they *both* have Negro ancestry. In the admixture of Negro and white ancestry, white characteristics tend to predominate. The child of a pure-blooded white person and an apparently white person with Negro ancestry is always white.

The phrase "coal-black" broods murkily over the whole troubled problem of race relations, but actually it is pretty much a figment of the imagination. Owing to the appetites of Caucasian males and the helplessness of many Negro women to defend themselves against these appetites, the Negro American is getting whiter all the time. The hypothetical white woman mentioned above, in quest of a "coal-black" baby, might very well have to settle for a brown, rather than a black, Negro, and would in all likelihood have to scrape along with a baby lighter than its father. The "black tide" of which so many Southerners live in such genuine terror is—seen from a vantage point that takes in the whole country—brown, rather than black. And it could not pass for a tide in any place larger than a bathtub. The Negro represents only ten per cent of our total population, and even if intermarriage were encouraged—nay, positively cheered on—in every state in the Union, the white race would not become dark. It would be the other way around. The dark race would ultimately become white.

When the canteen's no-discrimination policy was first proposed and the less hardy spirits murmured that there would be "trouble," the word "trouble" turned out, upon inspection, to mean two things—race riots, and the begetting of "coal-black" babies upon white Junior Hostesses. Both forebodings proved groundless. For security reasons, the military authorities requested the canteen to make a ruling that its hostesses should not go out with servicemen they met there, and the canteen, having the girls' anxious parents on its mind, was glad to comply. As a matter of fact, under our present social setup, it takes more courage than most young white girls have to go out on a date with a Negro. Old white girls, either, so far as that goes. Our Junior Hostesses were expected to talk to and dance with any serviceman, regardless of race, creed or color, who was not drunk or otherwise offensive. But courtesy is not copulation, as all courteous people know, and none of our white Junior Hostesses had to go home to Papa with an interracial baby wrapped up in an old plaid shawl.

IV

Color Line and Stag Line

————

WHILE THE canteen's no-discrimination policy
did not result in "trouble," its launching and
maintenance were a little more taxing than rolling
off a log. Any realist has to concede that—democracy or no democracy—at this point in the history of
these United States, you could not just invite Negro
servicemen into your canteen and call it a day. If
the no-discrimination policy had behind it the highest ideals of American thought and feeling, it had
in front of it a veritable miasma of legends, myths,
fairy tales and sweeping but inaccurate generalities.
This meant work. Not exciting work. Nothing on
the line of John Brown at Harpers Ferry. Only rela-

tively tame and minor activities like making phone calls, writing letters, talking to servicemen, interviewing Junior Hostesses, and holding meetings. But there were times when some of us used to think wistfully that old John Brown has a pretty soft touch, with nothing to do but loll around in that grave and molder, while we drudged away on committees.

One thing, though, contributed to make things easier, and that was the fact that we were working as a group. Except worry, there is very little that a single individual, working alone, can do about improving race relations in this country. The only way to make progress is to work with other people. All, or even some, of the tenants of an apartment house have a much better chance than a single tenant to secure the use of the front, instead of the freight, elevator for a Negro guest. A solitary individual is beaten before he starts if he tries to take a Negro friend into almost any of our restaurants.* I know, however, of a large organization which entertained a Negro writer in a midtown restaurant by the simple expedient of threatening to boycott the place, which was extensively patronized by the organization's personnel, if the Negro was not served and no nonsense about it.

---

* In New York State, a Negro may sue if he is denied service in a hotel or restaurant on account of his color, but this is a rather long-drawn-out way to get a bite of lunch.

One of the less dismaying aspects of race relations in the United States is that their improvement is not a matter of a few people having a great deal of courage. It is a matter of a great many people having just a little courage. And surprisingly enough, every once in a while the attempt to secure equality for our Negro compatriots turns out to be almost ludicrously easy. It only needed, it seems, trying.

I maintain against all comers that mine is not a sheltered life, and one of the arguments I adduce in support of this thesis is the number of people who have clawed at my elbow and inquired heatedly, "Do you mean to tell me those white girls were *forced* to dance with Negroes?" The answer is no. Our Junior Hostesses were not forced to dance with Negroes. The Junior Hostesses knew before they started working at the canteen that they were expected to dance with any well-behaved serviceman who asked them. If they could not whip themselves up to this pitch of impartiality, they were entirely free to go and be hostesses at some other canteen. It was easy enough, unfortunately, to find canteens where the uniform of the United States was not enough to gain a man admission.

Before she came to work for us, each Junior Hostess was interviewed by the Junior Hostess Committee and the no-discrimination policy was explained to her. Part of this interview was conducted

23

on bended knee. This was the part where the Committee implored the applicant, if she had any doubts about nondiscrimination, to speak now or forever after hold her peace. The canteen had approximately a thousand Junior Hostesses, but owing to the high turnover characteristic of all volunteer organizations, it was necessary to interview—in the course of four years—about four thousand girls. Of this number, approximately ten refused to work in our canteen on hearing that they would be expected to treat Negro servicemen just like any others. Sometimes girls were interviewed and then never showed up for work, but whether this was because of the no-discrimination policy or for other reasons, we had no way of knowing. Occasionally, we heard of young ladies who were quoted as saying they would not come to work for us because we admitted Negro servicemen, but there were always girls who wanted to be hostesses at the canteen, so the Junior Hostess Committee listened to these reports with great composure.

Not all the girls were Southerners who refused to work for us because we entertained Negro guests. On the contrary, there were some young Southern girls acting as Junior Hostesses whose ability to grasp the nettle and come to terms with reality was worthy of a twenty-one-gun salute. I had one of these on my own shift—a pretty and a darling creature, a veritable sugarplum. When this girl was

24

interviewed and told she would be expected to dance with Negro servicemen, she said with commendable honesty that she didn't know whether she could do it, but she would try.

Our dance floor, as a rule, was very crowded, and the hostesses were cut in on every few steps. But one night shortly after my pretty Southerner came to us, I noticed that the floor was not crowded, nobody was cutting in, and my little Southerner was dancing with a Negro Coast Guardsman. She was a beautiful dancer, and so was the Coast Guardsman. They were footing it very deftly, but intuition told me that the girl was desperately frightened. I improvised a series of lavish prayers that somebody would go and cut in, but nobody did. I didn't want to go and disengage her myself, with some invented excuse, for fear the Coast Guardsman would think I was detaching her because he was a Negro. It was almost a quarter of an hour before the orchestra arrived at an interval and stopped playing, during which time I stood at the edge of the floor, waiting to catch her if her knees should buckle. But she didn't miss a step. It was one of those superb exhibitions of good manners for which the South is justly famous.

Some time later I asked this girl whether dancing with Negroes had become any easier, now that she had actually done it and emerged intact and unharmed. I explained that the canteen did not aim to torture people, that we thought her an admirable person, and that if she wanted to leave, she could certainly go with our blessing. But she said that she would stay. I often think of her when I hear Northerners making sweeping denunciations of the South —especially Northerners who have never done anything about race relations except read books, and possibly not even that.

Unfortunately, a single interview, even when conducted by persons who have become thoroughly experienced at it, does not change people's characters. Our Junior Hostesses were young and flexible and adapted themselves quickly to new ideas, but in so large a number there was bound to be a small but irreducible percentage who would promise to support the no-discrimination policy because they wanted to work at the canteen, and who, when they actually got there, ignored or avoided the Negro servicemen. Sometimes—so vastly capable is the human mind of self-delusion—these girls even complained to white servicemen that they were compelled to dance with Negroes.

The Junior Hostess Committee watched for these people, and if no amount of talking and persuasion made them see the error of their ways, they were ultimately asked to leave. But before they were caught up with, they did a certain amount of damage. This was unavoidable. The no-discrimination policy worked, but it did not work perfectly. Once in a while Negroes were insulted in the canteen, sometimes deliberately and sometimes unconsciously. But the supporters of the policy were starry-eyed idealists, and it takes a starry-eyed idealist to accept disappointments and stay the course anyway. The beady-eyed realists are more childishly demanding, and go off in a pet the first time anything goes wrong. As for the Negro servicemen themselves, our belief—which was documented by letters they wrote to us—was that they preferred to take the risk of an occasional tasteless or callous remark rather than have us operate a discriminatory canteen.

The canteen held occasional meetings of all its workers at which the no-discrimination policy was discussed and overhauled, but the Junior Hostesses by far outnumbered all the other workers put together and had the most direct contact with the servicemen, so the policy succeeded or failed pretty much in accordance with their attitude toward it. This put a lot of responsibility on the captains of the various shifts of Junior Hostesses. Human nature being as infinitely variable as it is, some captains were more deeply interested in race relations than others, but all of them did a good deal of work on the problem. They held meetings of the girls on their shifts, at which the hostesses' minds were refreshed on the basic principles of democracy and the various problems that arose in connection with the no-discrimination policy were talked over. In addition, the captains were supposed to watch for girls who side-stepped their responsibilities to **Negro** servicemen and to deal with these girls in whatever way seemed best.

The captains were in a position to do some effective educational work, if they wanted to, and many of them wanted to. One thing that kept them busy was the high turnover of personnel previously mentioned. In one way, this turnover was good. It meant that many more people were reached than would have been reached if we had had a permanent, unfluctuating staff. But it also meant that the captains—and the other people concerned with the no-discrimination policy—found themselves saying the same things over and over, ad infinitum ad nauseam, to successive batches of new workers. To veteran workers, too, for that matter. People do not get over prejudice in one luminous flash of enlightenment. It is necessary to keep endlessly coaxing, cajoling, wheedling, encouraging and persuading them to submit their notions and fancies to the test of real, factual experience. The no-discrimination policy did not cause "trouble," but it must be freely admitted that it required the patience of a saint. In fact, saints were known to slink off and have ulcers while we were still in there hoarsely explaining that there is nothing in Christian brotherhood for a person to be afraid of.

The meetings of their respective shifts held by the captains were important to the smooth working of the no-discrimination policy. These meetings gave the hostesses a chance to compare notes and pool experiences. They digested their experiences by talking about them. Sometimes the captains read letters the canteen received from Negro servicemen, saying how much the canteen's policy had meant to them, so the hostesses would have a chance to realize that they were not working in a pious vacuum, but were embarked on something that had meaning and significance in other people's lives. Primarily, however, the meetings gave the hostesses a sense of not being alone, and sometimes girls too shy and timid to face the issues of race relations by themselves could take heart of grace from the security of the group.

One of the first topics that always came up at these meetings was the problem of "rescuing." It sometimes happened that when a Negro serviceman asked a white girl to dance, a white serviceman would cut in immediately and announce to the girl that he had come to "rescue" her. How to reply to these self-starting Galahads was always the subject of considerable discussion. Actually, no hard and fast rule could be laid down. It depended on the individual girl. The caliber of female on my shift ranged all the way from mature and well-balanced hostesses who were completely at home in a democracy to self-absorbed, flighty little chits who talked to Negro servicemen only if they thought I had my steely eye upon them. The canteen expected any girl to state, to "rescuers," that we made no differentiation in our treatment of servicemen and that "rescues" were unnecessary.

If the girl cared to take it any further, that was all to the good. But two painful lessons forced their way into my consciousness during my spell at the canteen. One was that you have to work with what you've got, no matter how unsatisfactory it seems. The other was that it is a waste of time to ask more of people than they have to give. Some girls simply did not have the intellectual power or the emotional stability to argue successfully on so dynamic and highly charged a subject as race relations. On the other hand, some girls did have. And some, bless their hearts, learned.

As a matter of fact, it was not very often possible to state to a prejudiced serviceman that the canteen had a no-discrimination policy and have the subject dropped there. Anybody who "rescues" a white girl from a Negro serviceman has a mind pressed down and running over with visions of "coal-black" babies, and these are thoughts he wants to share with all and sundry. At the meetings I had with my Junior Hostesses, the main part of the discussion usually revolved around Southern servicemen. Not all prejudiced servicemen were Southerners, but the non-Southern ones generally limited themselves to a sour remark or two and let it go at that. Southerners, though, love to talk. They like to talk about any-thing, but especially and in particular they like to talk about Yankees and Negroes.

Nothing venture, nothing gain. If you embark on a project as magnificent in concept as the brother-hood of man, it is foolish not to anticipate difficul-ties of proportionate magnificence. There must have been some Southern servicemen—it would be im-possible to guess how many—who came and went at the canteen without making any comment on its race-relations policy. Others, literally reeling from the shock of seeing a white girl sitting at a table with a Negro man, wanted to discuss the phenome-non in explosive and hysterical language. By persons who understood that these Southerners *had* had a shock, and needed reassurance rather than baiting, they could be handled without too much difficulty.

Once in a while, however—not often, but once in a while—a denizen of Dixie turned up whose white-supremacy tenets did not sufficiently disguise a na-ture akin to the beast. Since they did not carry their shootin' arns with them, there was nothing drastic these characters could do. Nevertheless, they were frightening. A Junior Hostess captain was once summoned to a corner of the canteen where three Negro soldiers and a white girl were sitting at a table talking. At the next table were five soldiers from an outfit which had a large contingent of Texans. The Texans, if they were Texans, were glaring at the

Negroes and allowing it to be known that where they came from, it only costs thirty-five dollars to kill the bastards. The white boys' voices were audible twelve miles out to sea, people were staring, and the situation was indubitably tense.

The captain used her head. With the speed of light, she rounded up every white hostess she could lay her hands on, and then she and the other white girls descended on the Negroes' table like rooks coming home at twilight. The Negro soldiers virtually disappeared from view in a cloud of white girls. For one long minute, the Texans stared in utter incredulity at this "white tide." Then, without a word, they got up and walked out of the canteen. The captain said later that in recollection, thinking of the Texans' stunned and slack-jawed faces, it seemed like rather an amusing stunt, but at the time she could hardly walk for fright.

I could well believe it. I was once sitting with a Negro sailor, when there suddenly materialized in front of me a soldier whose appearance suggested the hillbilly rather than the phantom of delight. He looked at the sailor and me with pure, blazing animal hatred. If I ever see that look again, I hope it will be in someone who is firmly anchored to a strait jacket. My Navy vis-à-vis may have been disturbed, but he did not show it. He kept on talking, so I took my cue from him and went on talking, too—though my heart was thudding like a piston and I did not have enough saliva to get me admitted to a life raft. The canteen clock being right over the apparition's shoulder, I was able to observe that he stood there for seven minutes. Finally, when neither of us paid any attention to him, he walked slowly away, keeping his head turned over his shoulder and favoring us with that maniacal glare until he was out of sight.

As I have mentioned, these people did not show up very often, and when they did, we always had *The Star-Spangled Banner* to fall back on. I have related the above incidents in order to be scrupulously accurate. With an enormous clientele of transients, such as we had at the canteen—and transients, furthermore, who had been ripped loose from their homes and other moorings and suddenly confronted with a highly uncertain future—it was inevitable that we should have an occasional visitor distinguished more for nervous instability than for polish and finesse.

But for every moment of strain caused by people like the hillbilly and the (presumable) Texans, there were hundreds and thousands of times when the canteen's interracial character impressed and educated white servicemen and soothed the raw nerves of Negro servicemen. These occasions were not marked by raised voices or any necessity for quick thinking, so they make rather colorless re-

33

porting. However, when Negro servicemen wrote and told us that we had given them hope for the first time in their lives, and when white servicemen wrote and said that we were the kind of people they were glad to go overseas and fight for, we knew we were on the right track.

V

Southern Discomfort

———

Perhaps it is because I am susceptible to a Southern drawl—my own speech sounds like hail on a windowpane—but I got to have a great liking for some of the Southern servicemen with whom I discussed race relations. I remember with especial warmth a sailor who came from Florida. He was a tall and well-constructed tar of thirty-one summers, with an engaging and likable countenance. Shortly after he came into the canteen, he saw a white Junior Hostess dancing with a Negro serviceman and went to "rescue" her. But the girl, suspecting a "rescue," said she had just started dancing with the Negro and asked the sailor to cut back in a few minutes.

Luckily, the Floridian's blood vessels were sufficiently elastic so that he did not have apoplexy on
the spot. But it must have been a near thing. He
came churning and boiling over to me and an-
nounced that he had not wanted to make a scene,
because that would reflect on the good name of the
South, but that he was bu'ned up. He'd just come
back from overseas, he said, and he wasn't fighting
so the nigrahs could forget their place while he was
away.

"Well," I said equably, "just because you fought
in the war, it doesn't mean you own it. My husband
is overseas, and he doesn't hold with your point of
view at all."

This gave the sailor pause. There was no part of
my husband's being overseas that I found refreshing
or joyous, but his absence did appear to lend me a
certain air of worth and solidity in the eyes of the
military. The pause, however, was not long. Pre-
cipitously, the sailor stated that there was a hospital
in England with six hundred Negro babies in it,
and I knew as well as he did (he said) that the mothers of those babies were white women.

I sighed resignedly.

One of the most monotonous aspects of race relations in the United States is the blind acceptance
—by otherwise sensible people—of any wild, half-
baked, fragmentary, unsubstantiated or even pat-
ently absurd cock-and-bull story that comes along,

provided it has to do with Negroes and sex. People who balance their checkbooks, tot up the slips from the grocery, count over the laundry when it comes back, and in many other ways behave with cool, hard-headed realism will turn out to be the suckers of the world when it comes to Negro sexuality. Nobody on God's green footstool could sell these people stock in a phony gold mine, but when the issue is sex and Negroes, they sit with their mouths open like fledgling birds and swallow whatever is dropped in. If white Americans conducted the rest of their careers with the same childlike gullibility they bring to bear on stories about Negroes and sex, a staggering percentage of our Caucasian population would spend its life in receivership.

My conversation with the sailor about his alleged English hospital was too long to be detailed, but in the end he was prepared to concede:

1. That he had not seen this hospital or these Negro babies. (He had come from the Pacific and had not been in England.)
2. That the person who told him this story had not seen the hospital or the Negro babies, either. (His inform-ant had also not been in England.)
3. That he had not heard anything on the radio or seen anything in print which could be construed as evidence that such a hospital and such babies existed.

4. That his informant had not heard anything on the radio or seen anything in print, etc., etc.

5. That until he could prove the Negro babies existed, and also prove that their mothers were white women, he was not entitled to use them as evidence of the sexual activities of Negro males.

"Look at the reality of the situation," I said. "You saw a Negro serviceman dancing with a white girl. She is not allowed to make a date with either him or you. Do you think he's going to ask her to marry him, on the basis of a few turns around the room? And do you think, if he does, she's going to say yes?"

The sailor was willing to grant that this was unlikely. He was also willing to grant that the Negro serviceman would not rape the white girl on the canteen dance floor.

"Well, then," I said. "Where's the harm? What's the danger? What is there to be so afraid of?"

"But you don't know how I feel!" the sailor said passionately, and plunged into some oratory about the carpetbaggers. I did not interrupt. Under pressure, when prejudices rooted in him from earliest childhood had been attacked head on, he had behaved with restraint, and he was entitled to blow off a little steam.

After he subsided, I said that it seemed to me his feelings were based on two assumptions:

(a) That Negroes are innately inferior to white people,
(b) That the first and foremost preoccupation of Negro males is to have sex relations with white women.

A great many people could be found, I said, who would agree with these assumptions. But a thing is not true just because a lot of people think it is. A lot of people once thought the earth was flat.

The sailor looked startled and was silent for a moment, but then repeated stubbornly that he was bu'ned up. Without prompting, however, he volunteered the information that he had been in combat with Negroes and admired them as fighters. He thought Negro servicemen ought to have the same treatment as white servicemen in every particular that did not bring them into contact with white women. I asked him what his program was for the Negro in America, and he said they ought to be left alone. He did not wish to see them persecuted, but thought they ought to be left alone to work out their own problems.

I couldn't help laughing a little.

"That sounds to me," I said, "like one of those uncomfortable and ridiculous family meals where Papa says to Junior, 'Tell your mother to pass the bread.'"

We talked for a while longer, and he appeared really to believe me when I said that the canteen did not enjoy upsetting and disturbing Southern servicemen any more than they enjoyed being upset and disturbed. When he left, he shook hands with me and said he was still bu'ned up, but added doubtfully that he supposed we were only doing what we thought was right. His last words were that perhaps it was all right up here, but I had better not try any of that stuff in Florida.

I said I wouldn't.

I did not convert the sailor. It is not my job, or anybody else's, to convert Southerners. Any converting of Southerners that gets done will have to be done by the Southerners themselves. No single individual, haranguing, can make a prejudiced person hit the sawdust trail. The modification of prejudice takes a long time, and occurs as the result of a thousand things that happen to the prejudiced person— things he sees and hears and reads, people he talks to, and places he visits. Any given reformer must be content to take a small and obscure place in a chain of cumulative pressures.

When my sailor from Florida left the canteen, he was a long way from being ready to let his sister work as one of our Junior Hostesses. But even in the most obtuse people—and the Floridian was far from obtuse—human consciousness is a sensitive and delicate recording instrument and takes the impress of every single thing that touches it. The sailor from Florida had seen respectable people, not shaggy-haired zealots, practicing racial democracy and continuing to be respectable. Not only respectable, but free from bolts of lightning and other manifestations of divine displeasure. That had become part of his experience. Whether he liked it or not—and he was both revolted and, in a dim way, attracted—he can never wholly divorce himself from it.

If I had to sum up in a single sentence my own experience of Southerners, it would be this: They do not have much fun. Admittedly, their rehashings of the War Between the States are tiresome. The moans and plaints about the scarred newel posts seem childish, in view of Coventry and Hiroshima, and the dents General Sherman left in the old family silver have pretty much moved over into the field of caricature. But passionately as many Southerners inveigh against the carpetbaggers, it is not really those long-dead entrepreneurs with whom they are angry. They are angry at something else—something they cannot put a name to—and since it is impossible to be satisfactorily enraged with an indefinable object, the quiet dust of the carpetbaggers serves as an excellent vehicle for their feelings.

The real cause of those feelings is not the dam-yankees or the carpetbaggers or General Sherman. The real cause is that, so far as race relations are concerned, history has caught the Southerners in a squeeze play. They suffer—and it is real suffering, too—from a mounting sense of suffocation. The rise in racial tensions in this country cannot be blinked by anybody bright enough to be allowed outdoors alone. The natural and very human reaction of prejudiced people—as the shielding tide of silence and indifference begins to ebb away and leave their prejudices coldly glistening and naked—is to look around for someone to blame. The Negro press or the Northern agitators or *somebody*.

Realistically considered, the rise in racial tensions cannot be blamed on anyone. We have fought two World Wars for democracy in the space of thirty years. In time of war, a nation gets very self-conscious about its national ideals. It has to. Otherwise its people wouldn't fight. Twice in thirty years Americans have rallied around the word "democracy," but when their glances fell on the Jim Crow section, they instinctively winced. Our two wars have given us a heightened awareness of democracy. But a heightened national feeling for democracy automatically produces a heightened outcry from the people whose habits of thought would be disturbed by the extension of democracy to the Negro American. So far as the rise in racial tensions is concerned, the point is not that biased people are becoming more vociferous. The point—and a very comforting one it is—is that biased people sense, and feel threatened by, a burgeoning of the national instinct for decency and fair play.

Prejudiced Southerners certainly require a measure of compassion, as having what is probably the most complicated headache any set of human beings ever fell heir to. The South cannot go backward to slavery, but because it accepts as real many fantasies and legends about the Negro, it is utterly terrified to go forward to racial equality. And this is only the half of it. Southerners have their fair share of the national instinct for decency, and that is what accounts for their fury at any suggestion that the Negro take his rightful place in our commonwealth. Only one thing makes people as angry as some Southerners become at the idea of racial equality, and that is the pricking of the angry person's own conscience. The Southerners are betrayed by that most infuriating of all treacheries, the one that comes from within. Something *in them* responds to the idea of justice for the Negro, and it is to hide that response—from themselves and from other people—that they kick up such a dust about the carpetbaggers.

They are fond of saying that if the muddleheaded Northerners and interfering do-gooders would only leave them alone, they could get along perfectly happily with the Negroes in the old, traditional framework. Aside from the fact that this is a somewhat lopsided sentiment, since few Negroes able to speak freely could be found to agree with it, it is also untrue. If the South were completely and utterly free from any criticism whatsoever of its setup for the Negro, it would be pretty nearly as terrified, confused and unhappy about race relations as it is now.

43

Though the crusading equalitarians fell silent, the tender Southern conscience would continue to nag.

Very often Southern servicemen, coming into the canteen and seeing Negroes there, made a beeline for the nearest canteen worker and exclaimed, "I'm from the South and I'm proud of it, and I don't like what you've got here." It was a temptation to reply briefly, "In that case, why don't you leave?" but that was too easy and irresponsible an answer. The serviceman's opening gambit showed vulnerability. If he had really been as confident of the essential rightness of his attitude as he claimed to be, he would not have gone about plucking at people's sleeves and defending himself. He would only have laughed, when he saw Negroes being treated without differentiation. "Those wacky Northerners," he would have murmured, and gone his way—serene with the heartless placidity of the moral imbecile. The angry argumentativeness of some of the Southern servicemen, though it was wearying to have to deal with over a long period of time, was a hopeful portent. It meant that their democratic training had not fallen on wholly barren soil, and that their sense of justice not only could be reached, but was already being nudged and joggled.

The main job of a Junior Hostess captain at the canteen was to keep her hostesses interested in putting their weight behind the no-discrimination policy, but once in a while a girl came along who

44

had to be restrained from embracing the policy too fervently. The younger ones, in particular—introduced to the notion of equality for the first time in their carefree and thoughtless lives—sometimes went hog-wild about it. They rushed right home and invited their mother's Negro laundrywoman to dinner at the Plaza. When the invitation was declined, they were angry and hurt. "You see," they said indignantly, "Negroes don't *want* to be equals." One had to point out to them that laundrywomen of any color do not generally feel at ease in the Plaza, but that the Negro laundrywoman might be pleased if her little girls were safe from being snubbed and taunted in public-school playgrounds on account of their color. Or she might esteem it a good thing if her sons were not barred from most American colleges, universities and professional schools on the sole ground of pigmentation.

The point cannot be too much stressed that in race relations, the single gesture and the single individual are more often than not doomed to failure. Only the group and the long-term, undeviating policy make much headway. Some of the Junior Hostesses grew weary and discouraged as Southerner succeeded Southerner and none of them beat their breasts and said, *"Mea culpa!"* in response to the hostesses' bright, beautiful and impeccable logic. But if you want to make the world a better place, the first thing you must accept is the fact that you cannot transcend your limitations as an individual.

On looking around at our world, there seems so much to be done that one wishes to be a thousand people, instead of just one. You cannot be a thousand people, but you can join a thousand people, and the whole will be greater than the sum of its parts. To a Southern serviceman, a single Junior Hostess advocating racial democracy seemed, at best, tetched in the head. But a whole shift of Junior Hostesses committed to racial democracy pointed up what the Southerner *must* feel before he can become less prejudiced—i.e., that relationships with Negroes other than the ones he is familiar with are not only possible and workable, but, in the long run, safer and more rewarding.

It is a mistake to try to oversimplify human relationships. Unconsciously, and in order to save time and energy, we often select one characteristic in somebody else and endeavor to make that characteristic stand for the whole personality. Except on the most superficial level, this trick will not work. Even the most seemingly one-faceted people are too complex to get along with, in any real sense, on such a narrow and arbitrary basis, and the attempt to do so always ends in bitter disillusionment on both sides. Profoundly shocking as are the things some Southerners say about race relations, there is more to the picture than that. From a practical point of view, it is not enough to sum them up—as some of the Junior

Hostesses did—merely by saying, "Aren't they awful!"

The Southerners say shocking things because they are terrified. They are desperately afraid that the Southern Negro, spurred on by men of good will, will turn the tables and make white Southerners accept the liabilities under which the Negro now labors. This is just a bad dream they are having. Southerners are so used to having second-class citizens around that they cannot imagine any civilization without such a group. Instinctively, but incorrectly, they figure that if the Negroes are not second-class citizens, then they—the white Southerners—will be. The actuality is that neither the Negroes nor the men of good will want white Southerners to change places with the Negro. These people want a civilization in which *no* group is systematically discriminated against, but this is an idea the Southerner has a lot of trouble grasping, because he cannot tie it up with anything in his background and experience.

The pragmatist—with his eye on the main objective of minimizing prejudice—has not one, but two reactions to prejudiced Southerners. The wish of these Southerners to corrupt American democracy cannot be allowed to go unchallenged. No amount of terror gives them the right to lower the ethical standards of the country and to cause those standards to fall into disrepute. But the pragmatist also understands that terror-stricken people are not pretty and do not behave well, and that the way to make them pretty and well conducted is to attack, not what they do, but the hallucinations which are responsible for what they do.

VI

"Start with the Learner Where He Is"

A FRIEND OF mine at the canteen once told me about spending two hours discussing race relations with a sunny and radiant little blonde, at the end of which time the blonde smiled ravishingly and said, "I think you're so right. I agree with everything you say. But I just don't like black."

This seems like a dampening little incident; but it, and others like it, had one comforting aspect. Prejudice does not exist in thin air. It is attached to people. You cannot get at the prejudice except by getting at the people. Talking with people who share one's sentiments is pleasant and restorative, but in the larger view, it does not accomplish much.

The very obstacles and setbacks encountered by the canteen's interracial policy showed that it was reaching the people who needed to be reached.

Owing to the high turnover of personnel I have mentioned before, interest in and co-operation with the no-discrimination policy went in cycles. I found it so on my own shift. Sometimes I had a batch of Junior Hostesses who were proud of the policy and alert to make it a success. Then these girls got jobs out of town, or fell ill, or joined their husbands at Army camps. Some of their places were taken by young ladies who, when they could not avoid it, gave lip service to the canteen's no-discrimination policy, but who did not really like or understand it.

The shift meetings were always attended by all the hostesses, both white and Negro. But on one occasion, when it seemed to me that many of the girls needed a little rosemary for remembrance of their obligations, I decided to have a meeting of the white girls alone. I wanted to see if I could get at the real content of their minds—a thing I knew there was no chance of doing with Negro girls present. The Negro hostesses, to whom I explained this, saw the point right away.

One of the first questions brought up at the meeting was whether it is or is not true that Negroes have a different smell from the smell of white people. That Negroes have a distinctive odor—which, it is always suggested, is offensive to white people—is a favorite argument of the people who want segregation. But what these people describe as a specific Negro odor usually turns out, upon investigation, to be merely the odor of poverty. Persons of any color who live in ill-ventilated houses, who cannot afford to send their clothes to the cleaner, and who eat the unbalanced diets of the very poor, are likely to have an aroma. However, it has not yet been proved, by either scientists or laymen, that there is one odor for white poverty and another separate and distinguishable odor for Negro poverty.

People who say they can distinguish a specific Negro odor do not mean they actually *can*. They mean they *think* they could, *if* they had the opportunity. Assume a mixed group of whites and Negroes, all of whom have had a bath and put on clean clothes at the same time. Assume an individual who goes up to this group, blindfolded, and is able to separate the whites from the Negroes on purely olfactory evidence, with no assistance whatsoever of a visual, auditory or tactile nature. Such an individual would be entitled to say that he is actually able to distinguish a specific Negro odor. But no such individual exists. Not so far, at any rate. Scientific research on the question of a specific Negro odor is as yet incomplete and offers no final and conclusive evidence either way. But in a book called *Race Differences*, by Otto E. Klineberg, the author refers to an experiment conducted by a scientist

51

who collected in test tubes a little of the perspiration of White and Colored students who had just been exercising violently in the gymnasium. These test tubes were then given to a number of White subjects with instructions to rank them in order of pleasantness. The result showed no consistent preference for the White samples; the test tube considered the most pleasant and the one considered the most unpleasant were both taken from Whites.

When the question of the alleged specific smell of Negroes was first brought up, by a somewhat embarrassed young lady, at the all-white meeting of the Junior Hostesses, many of the hostesses were startled. But as the discussion progressed, it was observable that they were relieved and comforted to have the matter brought out into the open. Quite often, well-disposed white people are haunted by the insistent folk myths about the Negro. They do not really believe the myths, and would not defend them, but are unable wholly to forget them. Thus these white people have a nameless, indefinite feeling of constraint in their relationships with Negroes and in their thinking about the race situation. An incredible amount of literature has been written about the Negro American, so it is fairly easy to consult authorities, and healthy, candid discussion of the old wives' tales and superstitions goes a long way toward breaking their hidden power.

The meeting of the white girls on my shift had a bracing effect, but bracing effects, unfortunately, do not last forever. The following year it once again seemed advisable to remind some of the Junior Hostesses of their responsibilities, so I called a meeting of the shift, and before the meeting, I wrote and mailed to the hostesses a memorandum on the subject of dancing with Negro servicemen. My object was to save time. It seemed to me we would cover more ground at the meeting if the hostesses had the canteen's position clearly in mind before they came.

The memorandum read as follows:

Quite a few of you have asked me questions recently having to do with the Negroes at our canteen, so I think I had better explain the matter in its entirety.

The canteen's policy about Negroes is based on a quotation which runs as follows: "We hold these truths to be self-evident: That all men are created equal. . . ." I'm sure all of you know where that comes from.

The canteen's policy about Negroes is also based on the 14th and 15th Amendments to the Constitution of the United States, in which it is specifically stated that nobody is to be denied the rights, privileges and immunities of American citizenship on account of race, creed or color.

One hears a good deal of talk, in some circles, about the Reds and long-haired radicals who want to tear down the Constitution. The Reds and long-haired radicals are

53

only spoken of as *wanting* to tear it down. The people who deny Negroes democratic equality actually *are* tearing it down.

I know that some of you on our shift are very deeply prejudiced against accepting Negroes as your social equals. You can't be blamed for having that prejudice in the first place. It was taught to you when you were too young and helpless to be critical. But you certainly can be blamed for hanging on to the prejudice when

    (*a*) you are now old enough to know better;

    (*b*) you are being given, in the canteen, a golden opportunity to come into contact with Negroes under the best possible circumstances and to find out what they are really like.

Let's examine the feeling that some of you have against, for instance, dancing with Negro servicemen and see what it really amounts to.

There is no scientific basis for the notion that Negroes are inferior to white people. A scientist, given a collection of human brains pickled in alcohol, cannot tell which ones belonged to Negroes and which to white people. You can check this statement in any good reference library. Intelligence depends on the number and fineness of the convolutions in the brain. It has absolutely nothing to do with the amount of pigment in the skin. If it had, you would all be much stupider when you are sunburned.

Actually, I don't believe any of you are very deeply

54

concerned with Negro intelligence. What worries you more is the fear of rape. You unconsciously, but very arrogantly, assume that no male Negro can so much as glance at you without wanting to get you with child. The truth is, that while you are an extremely attractive group of young women, there isn't one single one of you who's *that* good. Negro males react to you no more and no less than white males. As women, you know in your hearts that men of any description respond to you pretty much as you intend them to respond. This is especially true in the canteen, which has hardly any points of resemblance at all to a lonely, moonlit shrubbery.

The real basis of prejudice against Negroes is economic and historical, not sexual or psychological. The people who talk about "keeping the niggers in their place" never admit this, because it doesn't show them in an entirely favorable light. Such people prefer to fall back on more melodramatic arguments, usually (1) the honor of their women and (2) the danger of a Negro revolt. Neither of these two arguments stands up very well under close inspection.

Revolt is a troublesome and dangerous occupation. People will put up with an awful lot before they resort to it. If the Negroes ever do rise in the night sometime and murder every white man south of the Mason and Dixon line—and perhaps some choice specimens north of it—it will be because those white men richly deserved it. But there's one way to make absolutely certain that neither the Negroes nor any other section of our population feel impelled to rebel. That is to see that they have nothing to rebel about. If Negroes have the same education, the same housing, the same jobs, the same opportunities, and the same social treatment as all the other citizens in this country—all of which things we promised them in the Declaration of Independence and again in the Constitution—they will have no more impulse to rise against us than redheads, stamp collectors, and sufferers from stomach ulcer have the impulse to rise against us.

The other argument, about the honor of our women, collapses even faster than the one about revolt. Women—ask the man who owns one—can take care of themselves a good deal better than they ever let on. The way to protect your honor is to be honorable. If white people stood, in the minds of the Negroes, for fair play and justice and real democracy, they wouldn't ever have to worry about either sexual or nonsexual assaults.

The real reason back of the refusal of some of you to mingle with Negroes at the canteen isn't nearly as romantic and dramatic as you like to think it is. The real reason has nothing to do with rape, seduction and risings in the night. The real reason can be summed up in two extremely unromantic little words: cheap labor. As long as you treat Negroes as subhumans, you don't have to pay them so much. When you refuse to dance with Negro servicemen at the canteen, you are neither protecting your honor nor making sure that white Southerners won't have their homes burned down around their ears. All you are doing is making it possible for employers all over the country to get Negroes to work for them for less money than those employers would have to pay you.

Do you find that romantic?

You don't live in a romantic age. You live in a machine age, and it's getting more machinery every day. In the old days, large groups of people could live out their entire lives without ever finding out what other large groups of people were doing. That is no longer possible. Unless you can deinvent the airplane and cause it to fall into general disuse, you are going to spend an increasing amount of your time mingling with Negroes, Russians, Chinamen, Patagonians, and all sorts of hitherto unfamiliar people this side of accredited lepers. You might as well get used to it here and now, on Sunday nights at the canteen. It will save you a lot of trouble later on.

In our world we have radios, telephones, bathtubs, aircooling, vitamin pills and sulfa drugs, but we no longer have any group privacy. We can no longer wrap ourselves up in the comforting notion that we are better than other sorts of people. Our own inventions drop these other sorts of people right into our laps, and we either have to get along with them or watch our inventions—along with a lot of other things we hold dear—go crashing into the dust in a series of obliterating wars. There's only one possible basis for getting along with other sorts of people, and that basis is equality. Real, genuine, three-ply, copper-bottomed equality. If we have any secret yearning to think of ourselves as a Master Race, we have only to pick up a newspaper to see that nobody is giving odds on Master Races these days.*

A few words of warning before I close. Don't be surprised if you find some of the Negro servicemen sullen and unresponsive and some of them aggressive and too responsive. The war has put the Negroes in a difficult spot. We need them in the war effort, so we've been forced to give them more equality than we were ever willing to concede before. They aren't used to it, and neither are we. There are bound to be awkwardnesses and mistakes on both sides. If there are, remember that they are inevitable and take them in your stride.

Try to be a little imaginative and put yourself in the Negro's place. When you go into the canteen, nothing worse can happen to you than getting tired or being bored. When a Negro goes into the canteen, he has no reason to suppose he won't be snubbed by one of the girls on our shift or openly insulted by a white soldier whose "superiority" has not been noticeably enhanced by rye with beer chasers. Naturally, the Negroes are nervous and very possibly may not behave with Chesterfieldian calm. You wouldn't either, under the same circumstances.

The main thing to remember is this: *the Negroes aren't under any obligation to behave better than we do.* They didn't come to this country because they wanted to. We brought them here in chains. They didn't write the Declaration of Independence or the Constitution. We

---

* This memorandum was written in the spring of 1943.

wrote those documents, and if we now wave them in the Negroes' faces and say, "Ha-ha! Practical joke!" we must expect to meet the customary fate of practical jokers. We kept the Negroes in official slavery until 1864 and we've kept them in unofficial slavery ever since. If you meet a Negro serviceman at the canteen whose conduct doesn't come up to your delicate and exacting standards of behavior, just don't forget this one thing—whatever he is, you made him that way.

As a matter of fact, you meet plenty of white servicemen whose conduct fails to enthrall. Few outsiders realize, but all of us know, that being a Junior Hostess and entertaining unselected strangers for three and a half hours is difficult at best. You only make it more difficult when you artificially set aside a portion of these strangers as targets for unreasonable, unscientific and undemocratic emotion. If you'd just relax and keep your pores open, there wouldn't be any "Negro problem."

Sending out the memorandum did save time. The meeting which followed was one of the best we ever had. About thirty Junior Hostesses attended, and it seemed to me they were a not-unrepresentative collection of American thought and feeling about our Negro compatriots. Five or six of the girls were completely unprejudiced; five or six were Southern girls who said they danced with Negro servicemen when asked, but that it made them "feel awful"; and the rest were neither prejudiced nor unprejudiced. They were girls who had had sheltered lives, and while they were not naturally lacking in either imagination or sympathy, they had no conception at all of the difficulties with which Negro Americans have to contend.

One hostess said that she herself thought the memorandum was fine, but she wouldn't dare show it to her mother.

"When we are children," I said, "our parents protect us. When we grow up, we sometimes find it is necessary for us to protect our parents."

It did not seem to me imperative, I said, to show the memorandum to her mother. She, not her mother, worked at the canteen. The fact that she worked there and the fact that she had received the memorandum showed that responsibility for the social order was beginning to pass out of her mother's hands and into hers. I suggested that she should accept the responsibility rather than try to toss it back into her mother's lap. The most effective work she could do for an improved democracy would be among her own contemporaries, who might reasonably expect to be alive long after the parental generation is gathered to its ancestors.

Concerning the memorandum, the Southern girls said, in effect, "I concede the intellectual strength of the argument, but it doesn't change the way I *feel*. What can I do about my feelings?"

The discussion on this point was led by the five or

six unprejudiced Junior Hostesses, who said that
you cannot expect to get rid of a prejudice over-
night. You get rid of it gradually, by a series of experiences, just as you develop a muscle through
exercise. It was suggested that the Southern girls
could make things easier for themselves by getting to
know some of the Negro Junior Hostesses. Another
suggestion was that they make a point of talking to
the Negro servicemen who appeared most intelligent, responsible and mature. The unprejudiced
hostesses pointed out that the Negro serviceman had
just as much stake in having a white Junior Hostess
at ease as she had in being at ease, and that, generally
speaking, he took pains to set up a good relationship.

The main point which the unprejudiced hostesses
urged upon the Southern girls was that, in interracial contacts, there are *two* people involved—the
white *and* the Negro. If you are busy thinking of
somebody else's comfort, you have less time to be
aware of your own discomfort. In one way, the hostesses said, it didn't make any difference whether you
treated Negro and white servicemen alike because of
a genuine indifference to color or because of a stern
sense of duty. In either case, the effect on the Negro
serviceman was the same. All he knew was that he
and his uniform and his part in the war had been
accorded the attention and respect they merited. He
went away feeling that, contrary to his previous experience, there might be something about his native

land worth fighting for. He went away wanting to contribute as much as he could, from his side, to straightening out the intricate problems of Negro-white relations. He became, from the Southern point of view, less dangerous.

Later on the memorandum to the Junior Hostesses was picked up and published by two newspapers and reprinted in the *Negro Digest* and the *Magazine Digest*. I received a good deal of mail about it. One of the first letters to arrive read as follows:

Margaret Halsey:

I have been shown your vulgar article in regard to white girls dancing with niggers which to most decent real Americans is the lowest form of degeneracy a white girl can fall. Your canteen is no doubt a Communist Front hangout and a cess pool of iniquity and degradation to which I would not permit my daughter to get within a block of for it might contaminate even the air she breathes that must emanate from such a putrid den.

To enlighten you upon your ignorance of American policy and principles be informed that the "All men are created equal" of the Declaration did not mean niggers, as all the signers were slave holders, and a nigger was property and not *Men*. The 13th and 14th and 15th Amendments were written in the Constitution by the Republican Party renegades of the North as the means to subjugate white people of the South for political and economic reasons and has nothing to do with your perverted American idea of dancing with a nigger or Social Equality.

You are a renegade white woman if you are a white woman and certainly no lady of refinement. There are many of your class here in New York City but most of them do not practice what they preach for their daughters. Between the Communists, Left Wing New Dealers and politicians together with some of the renegade nigger loving newspapers like P M and The Daily Worker all angling for nigger support at the expense of white dignity and supremacy, and with white trash and scum like you and other hypocritical renegades supporting the nigger against white people I can only pray for the coming of the good old Ku Klux Klan—then the like of you will be tarred and feathered as you deserve.

A REAL PURE WHITE AMERICAN

This was the only abusive letter I received about the memorandum. I have always suspected that the writer was someone who first saw the light of day in a Teutonic province. By an odd slip of the tongue, the letter speaks of my perverted *American* idea of equality.

A number of people wrote me long, single-spaced, typewritten documents designed to justify the South's traditional arrangements for its Negro citizens. These correspondents, while clearly not regarding me as the apple of their eye, signed their names and addresses and kept their perturbation within the bounds of decency.

Most of the mail was favorable. The two following letters are fairly typical. The first was written by a Negro corporal.

My Dear Lady:

Army regulations make it imperative to state my name, rank and Army serial number. Let me begin this letter to you by saying first of all that I wish this were not so. The comrades of mine—here in the Army—and those many, many more in civilian life who I know would approve of the things I am about to relate, are important. I am not. I am just a cluck. But I still remember some of my former civilian traits as a social human being. One of the most important of them was to say thank you for any personal favors or democratic kindnesses bestowed upon my people. Some of them forget (but mean well) that the Negro's friends are people of rare courage and great understanding and insight. Let me include them also in my letter, please. I am an American of color, with an American Negro outfit.

My buddies in this outfit have many pals abroad and back in the States, too. They all speak so *beautifully* of their humane reception and subsequent treatment at your canteen. They all tell us it is a great spot, and we believe it. Its fame has traveled into many lands and been heard about upon more battlefronts than you would ever imagine. It has done much to warm the hearts of these men who—if, as and when they die—give up their lives for the Klan, the Gerald L. K. Smiths, the Rankins, the Bilbos and the rest of intolerant, blind, Fascist, undemocratic America, as well as for the finer element. Nobody says, "Has this guy kicked the bucket for so-and-so?", because he really didn't. He "kicked it" for America—the good, the bad, and the indifferent.

We can take it. But we are so glad to know that at home there are a few brave souls that want to put into practice those four freedoms of the Atlantic Charter which we are writing down with our life's blood. Keep up the good work. And know that over here there are a lot of fellas like me who can but say: These are the ideas, the things, the people who make me feel proud of my American heritage. Our battle goes easier as a consequence. May God bless you.

This one came from a white sergeant.

Dear Miss Halsey,

I have just finished reading an article written by you, and published quite a few weeks ago. You will probably understand this belated letter inasmuch as there are quite a few miles between the canteen and Tunisia.

After reading about the numerous race riots back in the States, you can realize how ripping mad it made many of us here in Africa. I've met and spoken to many of the

Negroes who composed active units that did heroic work at the height of the campaign in Africa. Nothing amazing about them. I won't be so silly as to call them Super-Dupers. They fight like any other American in the field. That, of course, is fast proving itself to be Super-Duper.

When speaking to Negro troops and realizing what a raw deal their people back home are getting while they fight for the country you get a funny feeling. You wonder whether that moronic white element that leads race riots ever stopped to question. Whether they realize that a bullet from an enemy gun does not stop in mid-air and inquire what color the skin is that it is about to penetrate. Bullets are about the least discriminating things there are.

. . . Among people who are "astounded" by these "alarming events" (race riots) you will often hear the comment: "I'm ashamed of white people." Perhaps when speaking to Negroes in uniform in overseas action, I should be "ashamed" at the behavior of my brother whites. Nuts on that. Too many of these people suffer from the "astounded" complex and while they express their "amazement" they peddle their anxiety to share the sufferings of the Negroes in their "hour of need" (a period consisting of the duration and six days from the time of a riot). . . . They almost want their listeners to cry for them, too. Then when the six days are up and you ask them to do something concrete to solve the problem, they give you an interested ear but balk at action. Pretty soon they're asking you whether you would marry a

66

Negro. I may sound cynical, but can honestly say I am not. Not when I know there are people like the ones at that canteen you wrote about who will risk being called "impolite" or "daring" for the sake of honest intelligence. . . .

VII

Up from Apathy

———

THE NUMBER of Negro servicemen entertained at our canteen varied according to whether there were Negro outfits stationed near or passing through New York. But on an average, about six or eight per cent of the servicemen who visited the canteen were Negroes—a proportion which was about the same as the number of Negroes in the armed services. People who heard of the no-discrimination policy sometimes asked curiously how the Negro servicemen behaved. These people seemed to have a preconceived idea that our Negro guests, discovering they were not going to be penalized for the color of their skins, plunged immediately into an orgy of arrogance and wanton rudeness. Actually, the Negro servicemen behaved just like anybody else. Were it not for the darker skins, you would not have known they were there.

Experience with people who generalize recklessly about our Negro compatriots has taught me to be cautious in making oversimple summations. Nevertheless, it was the impression of many of us who worked on the canteen's no-discrimination policy that the Negro servicemen, taken by and large, behaved a little better than the white servicemen. We found that both Negro civilians and Negro servicemen were willing to go more than halfway in cooperating with people whose good faith they believed in. But good faith, to them, meant action—not vague, unimplemented talk about how it is all going to be a matter of education.

A nation conditioned by soap operas and B pictures may not see sermons in stones and books in the running brooks, but it tends to see drama in everything. Interracial projects, in particular, are imagined—by people who have never been within a mile of one—to be uninterruptedly tumultuous. In practice, there is nothing especially dramatic in people getting along well together. As a spectacle, it is rather tame. The canteen considered that a Negro serviceman who was good enough to die for a white girl was good enough to dance with her. This reasonable—and, indeed, almost mathematical—concept came as a shock, sometimes, to people who heard about it. But the thing that shocked them was what went on in their own minds, not what went on at the canteen.

Some of my white Junior Hostesses preferred to dance with Negro servicemen because, the girls said, the Negroes were better dancers than the white boys. I took the hostesses' word for it, although the first Negro I ever danced with not only—contrary to popular belief—had no rhythm in his soul, but appeared to be wearing brass knuckles on his toes. However, he was an aged party of thirty-seven and perhaps in his carefree youth he was a less punitive dancer.

As for the Negro servicemen themselves, they did not seem to be overwhelmed by the opportunity to dance with Caucasian ladies. Once in a while a Negro serviceman would select the blondest girl on the dance floor and go twirling away with a "Virginia-was-never-like-this!" expression on his face. But most of our Negro guests appeared to prefer the company of the Negro Junior Hostesses, and the Negro hostesses told me that, as a rule, a Negro serviceman did not ask a white girl to dance unless he had a particular reason. Either she was an exceptionally good dancer or else she was someone he had gotten to know and wanted to talk to.

"This is the very first time I have ever felt and been treated like a man," a Negro serviceman once said to one of our workers, and similar sentiments were echoed in hundreds of letters the canteen received from Negro boys in the armed forces. But what the Negro servicemen liked about the canteen was not dancing with white girls, per se. What they liked was being free to choose with whom they would dance.

Maintaining this freedom for our Negro guests was a job requiring care, thought and a degree of dedication, and after the canteen had been in operation for some time, one of the Negro Junior Hostesses suggested that a special Race Relations Committee be formed to deal with the problems arising from the organization's interracial policy. The suggestion proved a good one. When a complaint was made that some of the women who directed servicemen to seats tried to segregate the Negro boys and to keep white Junior Hostesses away from them, the Committee investigated.

Incidentally, the Race Relations Committee was sometimes called upon to handle situations in which oversensitive Negroes or overzealous whites had seen discrimination where it did not exist. Another job was to deal with a few of the very light-colored Negro girls who were popular with white servicemen and tried to avoid dancing with boys of their own race. If you belong to a minority as systematically humiliated as our Negro one, it is certainly natural and instinctive to try to dissociate yourself from it as much as you can. But for the sake of the general *esprit de corps,* these instances of discrimination, though easily understandable, had to be coped with.

The problem of our Negro stag line was solved by a stroke of luck. Through an instinct heartbreaking in its implications, the Negro servicemen tended to collect all together on the stag line. The place where they congregated was a corner where they had their backs to a wall. We compel our Negro citizens to live en masse in places like Harlem, and then white persons who ride through Harlem exclaim, "Dear me, what a lot of colored people!" and conclude that the country is flooded with Negroes. These observers forget about the thousands and thousands of square miles in this scarcely diminutive nation where Negroes are not permitted to live at all.

Our Negro stag line not only suggested to unprejudiced people that the canteen had a Jim Crow policy, but it startled prejudiced people more than they would have been startled had these Negro servicemen been spaced more evenly around the dance floor. The Race Relations Committee was still struggling unsuccessfully with this difficulty when the canteen was redecorated and rearranged and the Negro corner inadvertently done away with. After that, we did not have a Negro stag line because there was no place for it to take shape.

It is not given to everybody to be able to conduct effective discussions on race relations, even with the

best will in the world, so one of the things the Race
Relations Committee did was to write down—together with the answers—all the questions and arguments which, in its experience at the canteen, were
likely to be asked about or raised against racial
equality. This document was furnished to the people
who had to conduct meetings involving race relations or who in other ways had a measure of responsibility for the no-discrimination policy.

For example, a question frequently asked by white
Junior Hostesses was: What shall I talk about when
I'm with a Negro serviceman? The Committee's answer was: The same things you talk to white servicemen about. Ask the Negro serviceman what he did
before the war, or whether he's ever been in New
York before, or how long it is since he's been home,
or any of the other things you ask white servicemen
in order to get a conversation started. A favorite
argument of prejudiced people is that if you give the
Negroes an inch, they will take a mile. The Committee replied by asking what is meant by "taking a
mile." If you offer a Negro a decent job, he will take
it. If you offer him a decent house to live in, he will
take that, too. But so would any white person not
mentally incompetent. It seems a little excessive to
demand that the darker brother spend his adult
years pretending to be feeble-minded.

Some of the arguments with which one grows
most wearisomely familiar, in working on an inter-

racial project, are not directed against the idea of racial equality in itself. They are directed—often by people who approve of racial democracy in theory—against the notion of doing anything direct and positive to bring it about. "But Negroes are snobs themselves!" these people said, endeavoring to persuade us that the canteen need not trouble its pretty head with anything as fancy and unnecessary as a no-discrimination policy. It is true that some Negroes are snobs. The Negro American has a social hierarchy of his own, based on the accident of color, and some light-colored Negroes will not live in the same apartment house with dark Negroes. But two wrongs do not make a right. The Negroes have just as much right to be snobs as we have; and the fact that we share with them a common weakness for keeping up with the Joneses, and for trading on arbitrary and accidental distinctions that have nothing to do with real merit, does not automatically free us of responsibility.

"There will always be prejudice, and there is nothing anyone can do about it, so why try?" This pronouncement, made with an air of hearty and complacent cynicism, is usually regarded by its owners as an example of fine Olympian detachment. And so it is, although fine Olympian detachment about things which are not personally inconvenient is a state easily attained by babies on leading strings and puppies in a basket. The assertion that nothing can be done about prejudice is suspicious in character, but it is certainly true that prejudice will always exist. So will sickness and disease, but that scarcely seems sufficient reason for telling our medical scientists to put on their hats, close up their laboratories, and give the spirochetes, bacilli and viruses a free hand.

Nobody with any pretensions to realism expects to obliterate prejudice and expunge it from the surface of this planet. But the complete removal of prejudice is not the issue. It is the business of churchmen and philosophers to go questing for absolutes. For the layman, the improvement of race (or any other) relations is a matter of degree. The task is not to do away with prejudice. From our present knowledge of human psychology, that is, at the moment, an impractical objective. The task is to narrow the field in which prejudice operates—to create more and more places, zones and institutions where people may not bring it in with them.

Projects like the canteen's no-discrimination policy, we used to be told—and by people whose motives were above question—defeat the very aim they are striving to accomplish. It is often maintained that such interracial ventures, by ruffling the plumage of our biased citizens, increase the amount of prejudice extant, instead of decreasing it. This same argument is frequently invoked against legislation designed to reflect in the laws of the nation our democratic ideals. But in whom is prejudice increased by practical measures toward a more effective democracy? Such measures *decrease* the anger, resentment and hostility of Negroes toward white people. One of the most important factors in the resolution of racial antagonisms in this country will be the morale, temper and attitude of our American citizens of color; but this aspect of race relations, although it constitutes one of the decisive elements in the problem, is almost always overlooked.

Visionary is the word usually applied to people who believe in doing something palpable and tangible about the improvement of race relations. But only two races are involved in the troubled question of our Negro minority, and blissfully to ignore the feelings and reactions of one of them is scarcely hardheaded or practical. The strongly prejudiced section of our populace is so unlovely, when aroused, that one is greatly tempted to soothe and coddle it. But yielding to this temptation can scarcely be justified in the name of practicality when, by pampering our biased citizens, we give our Negro compatriots so much cause for righteous anger that they prepare to take up arms and build barricades in the streets.

We have spent good money to instruct all the schoolchildren in this country, Negro and Caucasian, that freedom is worth fighting for. That instruction is a *fait accompli*. It is too late now to wish we had been a little more sparing with it. Many sweeping generalizations have been made about the Negro American, but nobody has ever claimed there is anything wrong with his hearing. "Then conquer we must, for our cause it is just," is not one of the most lyric lines that ever came out of America, but it is one of the most deeply, profoundly and inspiringly familiar.

From a common-sense viewpoint, practical steps toward racial democracy do *not* increase the prejudice of prejudiced people. They only make it more articulate. You cannot increase the amount of water in a cup which is already brimming over. If you add more water, you agitate the surface, but the amount of fluid in the vessel remains the same. Take the gloomiest view possible of democratic legislation and interracial enterprises, and you still break even, because what inspires the strongly prejudiced group to more violence inspires the Negro group to less. Actually, it is better than an even break. Strongly prejudiced people do not become less biased if you leave them alone, but mildly prejudiced people and lethargic people become more broad-minded and more interested if they have a chance to mingle with Negro Americans in the equality of work and play and of common problems and common interests. It is in the mildly prejudiced and the lethargic, who far outnumber the hotheaded diehards, that the hope of a democratic working out of our racial difficulties lies.

77

The supporters of the canteen's no-discrimination policy were accustomed to being told that interracial ventures like theirs are star-crossed and hopeless "because you can't go against the will of the people." In this connection, the Prohibition Amendment is always cited. But there are Jim Crow laws in South Carolina and no Jim Crow laws in New York, and which is to be taken as the will of the people? So far as our Negro minority is concerned, the will of the people has not yet revealed itself. The strongly prejudiced and the strongly unprejudiced are still in the process of trying to garner adherents. Nobody knows, as yet, what the will of the people is going to be.

Reluctance to stir up the emotions of the Negrophobes is certainly a natural feeling and one that can readily be sympathized with. But a democracy has the right to maintain itself as a democracy, and a nation sometimes has to discipline its citizens as a parent does a child, and for the same reason. Few parents or educators would maintain that when a child throws soup in his father's face, he must not be reprimanded or punished because that would only increase his desire to throw soup. Reprimanding or punishment will certainly provoke the young one into screaming that he is going to throw soup whenever he wants to. But a wise parent—however much he understands childish aggressions and sympathizes with childish difficulties in adjusting to the grown-up world—realizes that the child has to live in a world where the use of soup as a projectile is not well thought of.

Giving full rein to a youngster's desire to fling soup not only impairs the quality of the family meals, but it is not, in the last analysis, a competent or effective way of preparing the child to be a happy adult. However formidable the screams and outcries of the strongly prejudiced, it does not seem—taking the long view—that we do either them or ourselves any service by permitting them to continue utterly undisturbed in their immature courses.

In any classroom full of children, or any group of people at a tea or cocktail party, there are almost always one or more persons who are on the fringe—who do not quite belong. Sometimes this is because of qualities in the wallflowers; sometimes it is because of qualities in the group. Any civilization, whether highly developed or primitive, has one or more of what the orthopsychiatrists call outgroups. Assume a completely cynical attitude and presuppose that man's low and contemptible nature makes the presence of conspicuous outgroups necessary, and it must still be admitted that the Negro American has had more than his fair share of being an outsider and it is somebody else's turn now. Viewed less cynically, the problem of a democracy is not to abolish outgroups—which may be to a small degree, at least, inevitable—but to keep them from getting too far out. When the outgroups begin to lose touch with the main body of the citizenry, the nation ceases to be a democracy.

The process of pulling in the outgroups is one that a healthy society must continuously be doing, to maintain itself in health, just as a healthy human being must continually put food into himself, to keep his efficiency unimpaired. As long as we have outgroups, there is always the risk that beautiful and valuable citizens—like one's self, for instance—might accidentally or purposely be exiled to them. Moreover, the exiles in the outgroups, cut off from the sobering influence of the main body, may in their isolation become queer, fanatical, bizarre and dangerous. Last but not least, while we maintain minorities in outgroups, we lose their vitamin content, so to speak—their potential contribution to the culture.* A society struggles to fulfill its best instincts, even as an individual does, and generally makes just as hard going of it. The fight against prejudice is an inevitable process. Man has been warring against his own lower nature ever since he found out he had one, and the battle against intolerance is part of the same old struggle between good and evil that has

---

* To take a somewhat lighthearted but not wholly unimpressive example—it is interesting to speculate on what Satchel Paige could have done for the Dodgers in their mid-1930's doldrums. (For the benefit of the lesser tribes without the law, Satchel Paige is a Negro pitcher believed by some sports writers to have been, in his heyday, immensely superior to any of the Caucasian pitchers in the major leagues.)

preoccupied us ever since we gave up swinging from trees.

It ought, therefore, to be familiar, but it does not feel familiar when you first engage in it. A sensitive and intelligent woman of whom I am very fond once told me that she had decided against inviting to her house, to meet some of her friends, a Negro who was a professional colleague of her husband's. "We would all have been too nice to him, and it would have been quite horrid," this woman said, speaking rather defiantly. She and several other people had lost the chance to meet someone interesting, and her decision had left her feeling guilty and uneasy, but I knew what she meant.

Even the most wholeheartedly idealistic people are usually uncomfortable in their first contacts with Negroes as coworkers or as social equals. For one thing, these people feel trapped. Democracy does not require that you *like* every Negro you meet on a plane of equality, but most well-intentioned people unconsciously assume it does. They do not know what they are going to do if their first Negro turns out to be vain, pompous, greedy, selfish, tiresome, stupid or in some other way unappealing. Actually, nothing more is required of them than is required when meeting white people who have these qualities. Democracy makes many taxing demands on its practitioners, but suspension of the intelligence is not one of them.

81

Another factor makes for unease in first contacts with Negroes as equals. So much fuss has been made about the Negro's pigmentation that white people accustomed to Negroes only as menials are tempted to stare fascinatedly at the dark skin. Aware of this temptation, and not wishing to seem rude, they do not look at the Negro they are talking to at all, or only peep at him furtively. In this way, all the play of expression that makes for a sense of easy communication is lost, and the resultant feeling is one of great constraint, as if you had to wash dishes or make a bed with splints on your elbows.

But Negroes know they are Negroes just as well as thin people know they are thin, or tall people know they are tall. It is much better to look directly and candidly at Negroes you talk to, even if you are a little bit afraid your eyes are popping or your thoughts are showing. After a while, your interest is caught by what the Negro is saying—either because of its actual content, or because of what it tells you about him—and you start reacting as you would in any social situation where no question of race is involved. This takes practice, and only comes with actual experience, but the sensation is rather like learning to dive. After a series of awkwardnesses, you suddenly and involuntarily start doing the thing right.

Unconsciously, and without in the least intending to, well-meaning white people—meeting Negroes as

equals for the first time—have a simple reaction to
the Negro's dark skin instead of a complex reaction
to his whole personality. Probably the greatest single
source of dismay to the race of man is the multitudi-
nousness of life. The one thing every human being
consistently tries to do, all his life, is to make and
keep things simple. To a certain extent, oversimpli-
fication is necessary to the process of living; but in
some directions it is impractical and downright dangerous. Where our Negro minority is concerned,
white Americans have done a job of oversimplifying
that must be almost without parallel in the history
of psychology.

Parenthetically, it may be added that Negroes are
much less likely to oversimplify about white people.
They cannot afford to. Their position in this commonwealth is so unsheltered that they dare not be
wrong in their estimates of what we are likely to do.
But they cannot settle back and relax and just enjoy
being with us. Bitter experience has taught them
that our good will—where it exists at all—is neither
safe nor reliable, and they must perpetually keep a
wary eye out, in case we turn on them.

One of my Junior Hostesses once came to me in
great distress because in talking to a Negro serviceman, she had inadvertently used the time-worn
phrase about the nigger in the woodpile. By way of
reassuring her, because she was shocked and dis-
mayed with herself, I explained that any individual

is not only the product of his culture, but the product of *both* the good things and the bad things in that culture. The individual may conscientiously espouse the higher elements in his culture, but he cannot help being slightly conditioned by the shabbier elements, and in even the most generous-hearted people, there is always a tiny residue of prejudice. In people who are willing to put their idealistic beliefs into actual behavior, this residue is never large enough to worry about.

What makes well-intentioned people ill at ease in their first contact with Negroes on a footing of equality is a conflict between two opposing aspects of the civilization that formed them. On the one hand, these people have been taught, and have taken seriously, the democratic concept of equality and the religious concept of brotherhood. On the other hand, they have also been taught—in a thousand tiny, subtle ways and regardless of whether or not they were brought up in the South—to associate dark skin with

Spirituals
Big feet
Irresponsibility
Deplorable (from the point of view of Anglo-Saxon restraint) taste in clothes
Uncle Tom
Aunt Jemima
Rochester

Pullman porters
Inexhaustible sexuality
"Coal-black" babies
Rape

There is not room for these two reactions—the democratic one and the popular-legend one—in the same person at the same time. Not, that is, if the person is to be at all comfortable.

The ideas about the Negro which spring unbidden to a white person's mind when he sees dark skin are simple stereotypes that were worked out a long time ago, by the interaction of Negroes and whites upon each other in an agricultural economy based on slave labor. That agriculture has long since fallen into comparative disrepair, and many Negro Americans have never been within thousands of miles of the place where it once flourished. We have the word of Negro writers that Negroes sometimes—how often, nobody knows—pretend to fit into the stereotypes, in their dealings with white men, when in actuality they know themselves to be different. The Negro American has to get along with us *somehow,* and we have an unpleasant habit of making trouble for him if he intrudes with explosive realities upon the dreamy current of our fantasies and old wives' tales about him.

Since nature sometimes copies art, it may be that some of the stereotypes are true, or partly true, of

85

some Negroes. Or some of the stereotypes may be true of all Negroes on some occasions, but not as a regular thing. However, the stereotypes are valid *only to the extent that—and for as long as—they constitute the real and actual character of any given Negro.* There is no way of determining this real and actual character except by firsthand experience within a democratic—that is to say, a modern and unstereotyped—framework.

In addition, it must be kept in mind that stereotypes are tricky things to handle. No human being, of any color or any conditioning, fits into one very well or for very long. And, within a democratic framework, no agreeable relationship with another person is possible that is not based on a tolerably accurate idea of what that person is really like—on, that is, a complex reaction to his whole character rather than a simple reaction to some arbitrary feature of him, like his skin coloring. The subconscious mind is impervious to reason, but it can learn through direct happenings. You cannot change your feelings by telling yourself you ought not to have them. But they can be altered, and sometimes surprisingly quickly, by putting yourself in the way of experience which gives you different feelings.

All human beings have a larger supply of emotion than they can safely contain within themselves, and in order to keep sane, they have to project both love and hatred outward upon persons, things, causes, ideas and institutions. This is a sensible and fruitful arrangement, except in cases where feeling is associated with objects to which it does not really belong. In those cases, it becomes almost impossible to handle either the feeling or the object—at least, in any workable and pleasing way.

For reasons largely economic, the pigmentation of the Negro has been made to assume a staggering measure of importance, but in reality it has no importance at all. In reality, the dark skin of the Negro is *neither* good nor bad. It just is, like air or water. When the races of man—Caucasian, Malay, Mongol, Negro, etc.—were evolving from the primeval slime, the place in which the Negro happened to evolve was the jungle of Africa. For this reason, he developed dark skin, to protect himself against the actinic rays of the sun, and wide nostrils, to scoop in more of the wet, clinging air of the tropics. That, and that alone, is the sole meaning of the Negro's coloration, divorced from its association with cheap labor in a cotton-growing South—an association which has spread, in some degree, all over the country.

There is another aspect of the Negro which has been weighted down, even for technically unprejudiced people, with feelings that do not actually have anything to do with it, and that is his comparative barbarity. The Negro did not develop a civilization in Africa comparable to those which were developed in the temperate zones because the jungle makes virtually impossible the two things which are necessary for a burgeoning culture—agriculture and communication. Even today, with all our technological equipment, we do not try to go through the jungle. We fly over it. And we do not try to farm it.

Although strong emotions have been permitted to attach themselves to it, the relative barbarity of the Negro is a phenomenon of no particular significance. When he was brought to the North Temperate Zone, he was not given the opportunity to participate in the North Temperate culture. It may possibly be that he is incurably barbaric, but so far it hasn't been proved. What evidence there is seems to indicate that with half a chance—which is about all he gets, even with the breaks—he can get as much out of, and put as much into, the Temperate Zone culture as the people who evolved there.

The word "prejudice" means prejudgment. To have comfortable relationships with Negroes on a footing of equality, well-meaning white people do not have to renounce their capacity for judgment. They have only to form their judgments on the basis of good and bad traits that actually exist in their Negro friends and fellow citizens, and not on the basis of good and bad traits that are said or believed or assumed to exist in American citizens of color.

VIII

Sex, Jealousy and the Negro

———

IT NOW becomes necessary to talk in more detail about sex. The race problem would seem to be primarily economic, since feeling about it runs highest in times of hardship, bitterness, fright and depression, when competition for jobs is most cruel. But if man is an economic animal, he is also a sexual animal, *and he is both simultaneously*. The economic and the sexual aspects of race relationships in the United States are inextricably intertwined. Some of our citizens—a touch more acquisitive than is recommended in the Bible—would like to keep the Negro as a supply of cheap labor. In a democracy, the wish to keep human beings and fellow men as a supply of cheap labor cannot be publicly, and seldom even privately, admitted to. It is therefore necessary to defend such a wish with arguments based, not on economic, but on sexual premises. (The premise, for instance, that Negro men have an obsessional desire to marry or to ravish white women.) By this expedient of concealing an economic motive with sexual red herrings, many well-meaning white people are confused. They are so deeply confused that, perhaps understandably, they recoil from the whole issue and leave the acquisitive citizens a clear field.

One of the things that accounts for this recoil of well-meaning whites from their responsibilities is that the subject of race is so overlaid with violent, melodramatic words and phrases. Well-intentioned white people leading uneventful, fairly well-regulated lives hear words like "lynching" and phrases like "race clash" and "race riot."

"Surely," they think to themselves, "this turgid and furious business cannot have anything to do with my undramatic life."

As a matter of fact, these phrases represent only those parts of Negro-white relationships which have gotten out of control, and in the long run the whole resolution of racial tensions in this country is going to depend upon the building up of uneventful, undramatic, unremarkable relationships between Negro and white people in the same general economic and cultural classes and with the same general problems and interests.

One of the words which most disinclines white people to experiment in race relations is the word "rape." Here again it is impossible to isolate the sexual from the economic angle. Southern servicemen who came into our canteen and talked to us about race relations used to get pitiably upset because they had gone away to war and left their wives and sisters alone in communities containing large Negro elements which had not been given opportunities to refine and improve themselves. Few of these servicemen could think of anything practical to do about the situation except bring their guns back from the war and shoot the Negroes. If, that is, the Negroes had assaulted any white women in the interim, which the Southern soldiers confidently expected would be the case.

This project always seemed to me a superlative example of inefficiency. The main objective is assumed to be the prevention of assaults on white women. Two factors are involved: One, that the white women *are* women, a condition for which there is no known cure. And two, that these women were living among a group of economically exploited Negroes. That the Negroes resented this exploitation was perfectly clear from the Southerners' fear that they would express that resentment in sexual assaults the minute the white males left for the wars.* Given two factors—sex and resentment. It is impossible to do away with the sex, so the only course remaining is to do away with the resentment. If the Southern servicemen had left behind them, when they marched away, some real, believable, tangible assurance for the Negroes that their lot in life was going to be improved and their human dignity respected, the white boys could have spared themselves a lot of worry. And as it turned out, the Southern servicemen fretted unnecessarily. The racial disturbances which occurred during the war took place in Northern industrial centers and had no connection with rape.

In itself, rape is not important. That is to say, it is not statistically impressive. The easily obtainable figures show that the incidence of rape is not very high among either white or colored people, and when it does happen, the act is almost always committed by someone with a psychopathic personality— a condition which has no particular reference to pigmentation. What is important is the *anticipation of rape,* and how this anticipation—this imaginary, not-real, not-yet-happened factor—fits in and dovetails with the very real and tangible and nonimaginary economic factors whose drive is to keep the Negro as a supply of cheap labor.

---

* Negro males from these communities were also being drafted into the Army, but this was a fact from which the white Southern servicemen did not seem to derive much comfort.

Before the Civil War, no such aura of sexuality and sexual arguments and disputations hung about the Negro as hangs about him today. Southern statesmen, arguing against freeing the slaves, based their argument on the purely legal concept of states' rights. The Negro was not aureoled with sexuality to the extent that he is today, because at that time, no such aura was necessary. Negroes were chattels. Once they had been bought, they did not have to be paid for the work they did, and their women could be enjoyed by white males as property. But after the war, the Negro became a worker who had to be paid for his work, and sexual forays against his womenfolk became sexual forays against women, and not the simple use of possessions.

Out of the unwillingness of various classes of whites to accept the new economic and spiritual status of the Negro grew a curious, twofold legend. This legend blocks at every turn the democratically intentioned people who try to do anything specific and real about securing economic and educational equality for their Negro fellow citizens. Part One of the legend asserts that the reproductive instinct of the Negro male has all the sweet amenability of a typhoon. In arresting contrast, Part Two asserts that "Southern womanhood" has no reproductive instincts at all. The truth is to be found, obviously, where the truth is generally to be found—somewhere in between. Meanwhile, the legend, which grew up

93

as a defense against the *legal fact* of the Negro's freedom, served three purposes. It gave the white worker, competing with a Negro worker for the same job, a big edge in securing employment. It gave the entrepreneur an excuse which people would listen to for keeping Negro wages down and limiting Negroes to menial jobs. Last, and most importantly, it frightened off the democratically intentioned people who might have been counted upon to intervene on the side of justice, had there been no strange, melodramatic, sexual factor involved.

A more deadly tool, for an economic purpose, could scarcely be devised than a sexual legend, because sex is a field where legends take root faster and hang on longer than they do in any other phase of human life. In sex there are no skeptics. Or hardly any. Many an American male carries around with him a profound sense of inferiority because he has found that he personally can never live up to the sexual feats he has heard recounted in Pullman-car washrooms or club smokers. In all his brooding about the subject, one very obvious aspect never occurs to him—namely, that his informant or informants may not have been telling the truth. The amazing naïveté and gullibility of human beings about sex is evident on every hand. Point to any woman at random and announce that she is rather free with her favors, and everyone will believe you at once. Point to the same woman and state that she is impeccably chaste. If you get any answer at all, outside of a bored yawn, it will only be the murmured complaint that your conversation lacks its usual sparkle. People want to believe that other people are sexually unconventional, and sexual legends are perpetually attaching themselves to individuals—sometimes on the most trivial bases, and sometimes on no basis at all. No basis in actual fact, that is.

Even more instantly and more pervasively do such legends attach themselves to readily identifiable groups. A lady seeking a provocative title for a book, some years ago, called it *Latins Are Lousy Lovers*— it having always been a major premise of American folk mythology that Latins are exceptionally good lovers. One of the things that contributed to the dissatisfaction of the American G.I.'s with France was that the soldiers brought with them to that country the American belief that all French people are ingenious and untiring copulators and that no French girl requires more wooing than is summed up in the word, *"Combien?"* When the Americans found that compliant French womanhood was fairly narrowly limited to professional lights of love who charged black-market prices, they were disillusioned and disposed to be spaciously critical of everything Gallic.

There is no legend among Americans about German sexuality, one way or the other, so the American soldiers approached the Germans with no particular expectations. The deplorable charity of viewpoint toward the Germans displayed by so many of our soldiers may have been due in part merely to the absence of keen disappointment. Incidentally, the American legend about French sexuality has not been noticeably impaired by the experiences of the G.I.'s. The soldiers' disillusionment was not of a kind they cared to elaborate on to the folks at home, and the legend continues to flourish, among the generality of people, with almost its original force.

The above examples are instances of sexual legends which have no economic basis. Or, at least, no profound and far-reaching one. The mythology which has grown up about the Negro and sex is a thousandfold more deep-rooted and complex and difficult to expose to the healthy light of day. This is partly because the Negro's pigmentation makes him even more identifiable than Latins and Frenchmen, but mainly because, in the case of the Negro, the sexual legend has been pressed into service to implement an economic drive. This economic drive, moreover, is particularly snarling and embattled because it is cutting across the grain of the national ideal of democracy and brotherhood. Thus, the very people who have most to gain from such a drive cannot themselves be easy in their minds about it, and must be unremitting in their attempts to justify themselves by talking about Negro sexuality.

Among the letters I received after the memorandum to the Junior Hostesses was published was a communication from a thoughtful and much troubled white woman who lives in one of the more opulent suburbs of New York. This woman said that she herself was wholeheartedly in favor of the canteen's no-discrimination policy, but when she discussed it with her friends, their invariable comment was, "You wouldn't say that if you had daughters, instead of sons." Or sometimes her friends said, "Young girls shouldn't be exposed to that. Though perhaps older women could talk to the Negro boys." These objections were typical of the ones that were often made to the canteen's no-discrimination policy. They did not come predominantly from red-necked hillbillies or creaky Southern aristocrats. Very often they came from people whose instincts were genuinely democratic, but who could not let those instincts go into full and complete operation because of the bugaboo of the Negro and sex.

"Young girls shouldn't be exposed to that."

Or, to put it more specifically, young white girls should not be exposed to the society of young male Negroes. Before going into the thoughts and feelings which lie back of this pronouncement, it would perhaps be better to explore the reality situation. In our canteen, young white girls talked to and sometimes danced with Negro servicemen. What happened can be summed up in one word: nothing. We did not protect the young white girls, because there was nothing to protect them *from*.

However, not to leave any angle unexplored, suppose for a moment that a Negro serviceman had been "fresh" or presuming with a white Junior Hostess. Suppose he was too free in his comments about her person or that he tried to pitch the conversation to a degree of intimacy she found distasteful. It seems, upon examination, a comparatively minor crisis. The white Junior Hostesses were not without experience in handling white servicemen who were too arduous in their advances, and when a man's biological drives begin to push him beyond the framework of accepted behavior, it is of no particular consequence—from a strictly practical point of view—whether he is Negro or Caucasian. He says the same things and he has the same approach, because there *is* only one approach. A white hostess would have had exactly the same problem with a too-insistent Negro serviceman that she had with the too-insistent white ones, and a hostess who could not learn to master the problem of the overimpetuous male, of any description, had no business working in a canteen at all.

One of the results of the memorandum to the Junior Hostesses was that after its publication I received letters from a great many Negro servicemen. Three of these letters—all from young men who had clearly not had many educational advantages—

failed to please. The writers, naïve and inexperienced, assumed that my interest in improved race relations carried with it a personal and sexual interest in them. Many Southern Negroes have been told by white Southerners that the interest of "Northern intellectual women" in improved race relations is not idealistic, but sexual—a device used by such women to secure Negro lovers. The origin of this bit of white folk propaganda is obvious. People who either have no idealism themselves or who have had completely to suppress it in order to maintain the Negro-white *status quo* find it utterly impossible to believe that such a quality exists in others.

I always acknowledge any letter I receive about my publications, and I acknowledged the three letters from these Negro boys, too. I thanked the writers for the nice things they had said about the memorandum, but added that I was a soldier's wife and under the strictest injunction not to sit under the apple tree with anyone else but him. All three servicemen wrote me sincere and rather touching apologies, and with two of them I continued to correspond until the end of the war. Most white people, whether prejudiced or unprejudiced, are much more preoccupied with their own reaction to the Negro than with the Negro's reaction to them; and because of this, many simple and reassuring truths about the Negro American get overlooked— one of them being that he understands English.

"Young girls shouldn't be exposed to that."

It is an indication of the white man's preoccupation with his own reactions that "young girls" always means "young white girls." But in our actual experience, running a nondiscriminatory canteen, the shoe was on the other foot. Too much cannot be said for our Negro Junior Hostesses. They were young women whose background and education entitled them to hold up their heads in any circle, but they had enough breadth of vision to be willing to risk encountering boorish and unmannerly people in order that the two races might have a chance to get to know each other better. While the backbone of the Negro sexual legend is that all Negro men want to sleep with white women, there is a sort of auxiliary myth to the effect that all Negro women want to sleep with anyone who comes along.

People in the grip of a legend are so unobservant as to be virtually blind. The unmistakable respectability of our Negro Junior Hostesses did not keep some of the white servicemen from trying the *"Combien?"* approach, though a child of four could have predicted the ensuing rebuff. "Come on, take us up to Harlem, we know how to show you a good time," was the most genteel way they phrased it. Once some white servicemen, talking to a group of our Negro Junior Hostesses, pulled out pictures of themselves taken while the white men were having sex relations with native girls in Trinidad. Our no-discrimination

100

policy certainly meant that we had to be alert to protect young girls. But not young white girls.

So much for reality. So much for the nonlegendary facts.

"Young girls shouldn't be exposed to that."

White people—even white people with democratic
impulses—are timid about letting Negro men meet
white girls as equals because they think the Negroes
will take advantage of proximity to ask the white
girls to marry them. That, at least, is what white
people *think* they think. Actually, this does not
represent their thoughts with entire accuracy. Marriage is not compulsory. Marriages are entered into
voluntarily. What the white people are afraid of is
not that the Negro men will propose to the white
girls, *but that the white girls will say yes.* The whole
implication behind the hackneyed old question,
"Would you like your daughter to marry one?" is
that your daughter *would* fall in love with one, and
marry him quick as a flash, if she got the chance.

In all the talk about Negroes and sex, the em-
phasis is always on how supremely desirable Negro
men find white women. But the real belief is exactly
the opposite. The real belief underlying the wish to
keep Negro men away from white women is that
white women, if they get to know them as equals
and can meet them without losing caste, *will find
Negro men attractive.* During the war, the United
States swarmed with canteens where young white

girls entertained white servicemen. The parents and guardians of these girls trusted them to work at those canteens without entering into rash or disastrous relationships with the servicemen they met. There were only a few canteens in the whole country where Negro servicemen were entertained along with white servicemen. Romantic relationships beteen Negro men and white women are penalized, in most circles, by ostracism of a fairly devastating kind. Since all human beings are by nature social and interdependent, ostracism is one of society's most powerful weapons for keeping people in line. But the parents and guardians of the white girls did not believe even the threat of ostracism potent enough to counteract the persuasiveness and attractiveness of Negro males, and to insure that the relationships of their daughters with Negro servicemen would be merely friendly and casual.

Almost all social situations involving people of opposite sexes and about the same age are potentially romantic. People who say, "Young girls shouldn't be exposed to that" infer that young white girls find the romantic potential distasteful when Negroes are in the picture. But if this were true, there would have been canteens all over the country with no-discrimination policies, because the relations between white hostesses and Negro servicemen could have been guaranteed to be completely sexless and unproductive. Whatever the Negro servicemen proposed, the white girls would all have said no.

If the people who clamor for segregation knew what they were revealing about themselves and, by implication, about the women they want to keep "pure," they would subside in an agony of blushes. For the real basis of segregation is not repulsion, but attraction. You do not have to put a wall between yourself and any object by which you are genuinely repelled. You can trust yourself to stay away from it without any wall. A man with no addiction to alcohol can keep liquor in his closet all the time. It is the drunkard trying to reform who has to give away every drop of alcohol in the house, because of the pull it exerts on him. The walls—social, economic and educational—which we have erected between ourselves and the Negro American were not put there because of a fear that the Negro would gravitate toward us. They were put there because of a fear that we would gravitate toward the Negro.

As it is popularly expressed, the legend about the Negro American is only half stated. The popular expression is that Negro men want white women. But the popular, though unstated, belief is that they not only want them, but they can get them, unless every barrier ingenuity can devise is raised. And even with all the barriers up, in every possible field —social, economic and educational—the people who erect those barriers have no real confidence in them. They are in a constant panic for fear the walls will prove inadequate.

In actual practice, the barriers are fairly efficient. Owing to the discrimination against Negroes in employment, white women seldom meet Negro men in the places where they work. So many difficulties are placed in the way of the Negro seeking education that not many Negro men—compared to the total number of Negroes in the country—are able to educate themselves to a point where they have interests in common with a moderately enlightened white woman. And even in the North, few white women have the courage to go about in public with a Negro escort and risk the intrusive comments of the vulgar.

The barriers erected by white people between themselves and their Negro compatriots are a dead giveaway. They are a monument to the deep-seated belief of white people in the sexual attractiveness of Negroes. In the final analysis, what segregation and discrimination and "keeping the nigger in his place" amount to is this: that white males never have to compete on a footing of equality with Negro males for *any* woman, Negro or white. And when people shrink from competition and arrange matters so that they never have to compete, there is only one possible interpretation: those people are afraid they cannot win.

Quite aside from all the whispered myths and

furtive folklore, the structure of American society makes it clear that white Americans believe the Negro American has got something sexually which they, the whites, haven't got. The obvious question arises whether this belief has any basis in fact and truth. In one respect, it certainly does. Not because of anything in himself, but owing solely to the misguided activities of white people, the Negro American has the very potent and compelling attraction of forbidden fruit. No white man in the United States can ever produce quite so intense a reaction, of any kind, in a white woman as a Negro male can, because the white woman has not been trained from childhood to believe that a white man is the one thing which, under any circumstances, she may not have.

This kind of education inevitably boomerangs. If you set aside a special group of men, and warn young women away from them on pain of crushing social punishment, the primmest and most acquiescent young miss in the world is going to have moments of suspecting that you are keeping those men away from her, not because they are especially bad, but because they are especially good. All human beings are instinctively curious, and those things in our civilization in which we take the most pride were developed originally because of somebody's instinct to explore. Where white and Negro children play and go to school together in unexciting equality, the

Negro male seems to the white female a common-place feature of the landscape. Her natural and healthy instinct to master the environment by exploring it is not baffled and frustrated, and her curiosity, satisfied, is at rest.

But when a caste system places the Negro male outside the humdrum environs of democracy, he becomes an unknown, half-legendary, larger-than-life figure swathed in the awesome and impressive draperies of taboo. In that position, he produces in the white woman a reaction that is simple and child-like, but devastating. He makes her curious. She wants to know. She wants to find out. "Is it true, what they say about Dixie?" Since her training usually compels her to suppress this curiosity, and not even admit it to herself, she very often hates the Negro for arousing it and thus making her tense and uncomfortable. But the white woman could be trained by the same methods to have an identical reaction to men with mustaches or men over six feet tall. The important factor is not the Negro, but the dynamic force of human curiosity and the distortion that ensues when it is denied a simple and natural outlet.

The question still remains whether there is anything in the Negro himself to justify the feeling of white people that barriers of every kind—political and economic, as well as social—must be erected against the compelling pull of his sexuality. Most, and perhaps all, white people take it for granted that Negroes are more musical, more rhythmical, better co-ordinated muscularly, more impulsive, more spontaneous, closer to the child and the pagan than white people are; and from this they infer that the sex life of the Negro is more uninhibited and more gratifying than the sex life of white people, with its hesitancies, shyness, self-doubts, misgivings, embarrassment and other hampering phenomena. People from Southern agricultural communities where the Negro population consists largely of farm workers living in extremely primitive conditions are vociferous in their contention that the life of the Negro contains sexual gratifications on a scale that would make white people blink. Certainly the belief is widely held, both in the North and the South, that Negro women respond instantly and enthusiastically to all sexual advances and that Negro males have sex organs which dwarf those of white men.

Before attempting to decide whether it is actually true, as most white Americans believe, that the Negro is more potent sexually than the white, it is necessary to determine what is meant by potency. Sexual potency is not a simple or a single thing, but a complicated phenomenon existing on several different levels. The American male who is troubled by the fact that he has never personally matched the sexual prowess he has heard about at stag parties overlooks the fact that such prowess represents potency only on the exploratory, self-absorbed level of the adolescent. It is comparatively easy for a man to be potent when he is being constantly stimulated by new mistresses to whom he is under no particular obligation and with whom he does not have to set up a relationship that will stand the test of time. But sexual potency with the same woman, over a long period of time, and in a relationship which involves common problems, common interests, and a real interplay of personalities, is much more difficult of achievement.

Human beings tend to think of their sex drive in a highly personal way. To them, their own sex drive seems unique, individual and distinctive, and they find it hard to believe that other people have one, too, and that the drive has common features in everybody. Even people who believe they do not have a sex drive feel its very absence is distinctive and peculiar to them. But viewed with detachment (if that is possible), the sex drive is one of the most impersonal institutions observable on this planet—a blanket impulse implanted in every human being in the world and extending even to the flora and fauna. What seems to the individual particularly distinctive about his sex drive is its strength, about which he is both proud and somewhat alarmed. However, the strength of the sex drive is a cause for rejoicing, rather than dismay, since that drive is our sole weapon against oblivion. It is all we have with which to counteract the effects of plague, disaster, pestilence, famine, disease and war, and it takes precedence even over the U.N. and penicillin. One comic feature of our Anglo-Saxon, Puritanical, Calvinistic, Victorian civilization is the number of people it produces who deplore the strength of the sex drive and fail to realize that, but for that baleful influence, they would not be here to deplore the strength of the sex drive.

The activities of primitive people are simpler and more direct than those of the larger and more complicated groups who somewhat recklessly describe themselves as "civilizations." Primitive women go barefoot, instead of wearing shoes with the toes and heels cut out. Primitives prepare their food simply, when they prepare it at all, and do not serve it à la mode and à la king. And although they have sets of rules about sexual unions, such unions are arrived at more frequently and more directly than is expedient in nonprimitive societies. By some of the people in complex societies, the much less trammeled sexual gratifications of primitives and pagans are regarded with open envy. In others, these gratifications evoke disgust and moral indignation. The comparison should not really call forth either emotion. Primitive and pagan societies and customs are neither better nor worse than civilized ones, any more than an apple is better or worse than a plum. They are simply different.

When a man in a complex society falls ill, he can usually find out what he has got, what it came from, how to cure it, and how to prevent its recurrence. When a primitive falls ill, he can do nothing but cower helplessly under the mysterious blight which he does not understand and to which he can oppose only chants and incantations. Primitives do not have fewer worries than civilized people—they have different ones. Things that seem to us completely natural and understandable, such as a clap of thunder or the fall of night, confuse and puzzle the primitive and sometimes frighten him to the point of utter demoralization. His sex drives are not hedged about with so many thou-shalt-nots, and he is therefore spared a large number of the nervous complaints so predominant in nonprimitive society. But he has other things to worry about. And if his sex life is simple and direct, it is not because he is immoral or degenerate, but because all the patterns of his life are simple—sex, as well as everything else.

In an intricate, technological civilization, all the patterns of life are complex. In such a civilization, much of the energy which the primitive puts into simple, direct gratification of sex is diverted into other channels—invention, exploration, art, wit, education, friendship, family ties, the prolonged (compared to noncomplex societies) care of the young. What is characteristic of the civilized man

110

is his ability to postpone gratification, in order to achieve a sense of power and mastery, instead of taking the most immediate satisfaction at hand. Reproduction being indispensable for the continuance of the race, the most immediate satisfaction at hand is likely to be reproductive in character. What is also characteristic of civilized man is that his activities are many and diverse, instead of few and simple.

Unfortunately, this arrangement does not work out perfectly for him, any more than primitive society works out perfectly for primitives. The family, in civilized society, is a much more sharply defined institution than it is in primitive societies. This is the source of profound and long-lasting emotional pleasures unknown to the primitive, but it also means that to preserve the stability of family relationships, the sex drive must be sharply curbed. Civilized man, therefore, has always to carry around with him a residue of unexpended sex drive. While he cannot be crushed and intimidated by a clap of thunder or the fall of night, unexpended drives of any kind do not tend to make people entirely happy. The civilized man, if he is honest with himself, regards the fully expended sex drive of the primitive with envy. If he is not honest with himself, he regards it with hatred. In either case, he overlooks the problems and heartaches of the primitive. In either case, he takes the part for the whole, and assumes that because the primitive's sex life is full of gratifications, all the rest of his life is equally satisfactory —which is an unwarranted assumption.

This seems like going all around Robin Hood's barn to answer the question of whether the Negro American is more potent sexually than the white American; but Negro-white relations in this country have reached such a state of confusion that to understand them at all, it is necessary to go back to the beginning. So far as I know, there are no reliable, scientific studies or surveys of the comparative sexual potency of the Negro American and the white American. No conclusion can be arrived at, therefore, except what may be inferred from observing the factors conducive, or not conducive, to potency in the lives of the two groups.

The sex patterns of a group or of an individual are all of a piece with the nonsexual patterns of that group or that individual. That is to say, if all the other patterns are simple, the sexual patterns will be simple, too. If all the other patterns are complex, the sexual patterns will also be complex. The patterns of white American society are complex. Achievement, both spiritual and material, at the price of curbing the reproductive instinct, is characteristic of that society. But the Negro American does not live *in* white American society. He only lives next door to it. Except as a servant, we do not let him into our homes, our churches, our schools, our

112

clubs, or any of those places where we are most completely ourselves and where, were he admitted as an equal, we could expect to exercise the most profound and noticeable influence on him.

In order to get his labor cheaply, we have forced a primitive life upon him. Achievement is not characteristic of Negro American society. So many obstacles are placed in the way of the Negro's accomplishing anything that even a modest achievement is difficult for all Negroes and for millions of Negroes it is downright impossible. It therefore seems safe to say that where simple nonsexual patterns of life have been forced upon the Negro, his sexual patterns will be simple, too. That is to say, in those situations where he is denied all outlet for his ambition and not allowed to prepare himself for accepting responsibilities which would drain his energies out of sexual channels, he probably has fewer inhibitions than the white American and greater sexual potency, on the adolescent level.

It is, however, inaccurate to make sweeping statements about a group of people and then assume that these statements are true of every individual in the group. While the Negro American is not *in* white civilization, he does live next door to it. He lives in the same country with it, and he cannot wholly escape being influenced by it. Furthermore, the influence of the white civilization is bound to vary from one Negro to another. Some Negroes are fairly closely involved with the civilization of the white man, while others are almost completely out of touch with it. And there are infinite variations in between. It has been my own observation, for what it is worth, that those Negroes whose lives are most like the lives of white people—whose education and responsibilities are most nearly parallel to those of the whites and who are most accustomed to mixing with white people as equals—also show signs of being conditioned by the white man's restraints and inhibitions about sexual activities.

If, as seems arguable, some (but not all) Negro Americans have more freedom from inhibition and greater sexual potency than white Americans, it must be remembered that the Negro has, for economic reasons, had that potency forced upon him. It is the argument of some apologists for the Negro-white *status quo* that Negroes enjoy living a primitive life in the middle of a dominant, nonprimitive society. In England, before the war, periodic attacks used to be made by tenderhearted people on the institution of fox hunting, because the fox, if overtaken by the hounds, is literally torn to pieces by them. "But the fox likes it!" was the passionate defense of the hunters. A primitive life, like any other system of living which will enable people to support existence, has certain advantages. Some Negroes, compelled to accept the primitive structure and unable to do anything about it, quite sensibly make the most of what they have. Whether they like it or not—whether they would deliberately choose it, if they had a choice—is something else again. The arrangements of their lives and ours are not such that they can safely confide in us. But the amazing record the Negro has made in overcoming his illiteracy in the last seventy years, together with the other advances he has made wherever he has had a chance, would seem to suggest that primitive living—whatever advantages it may have on a remote tropical isle —is not a comfortable thing to have forced upon you in the middle of a large, modern, industrial country.

One of the Junior Hostesses on my shift was a very light Negro girl, just out of college, who had an ethereal, Madonna-like beauty and a character to match. She was, and still is, one of the sweetest and most rewarding human beings I have ever known. One night a white serviceman asked her to dance, and when he got her out on the floor, where the light was stronger, he said, "My God, a nigger!" and walked away, leaving her standing alone among the dancers. At another time, I had two Junior Hostesses who were employed by the same company. They were both vital and attractive girls. One was white and one was a Negro. After they had been working together for three months, they each got a raise, but the white girl's raise was double the Negro girl's and it was admitted with careless frankness that the distinction was solely on the basis of color.

No white person, even when he wants to, can understand what it means to be a Negro living in the United States of America, any more than a non-combatant can understand what it means to be in action. The constant danger which enshadows the Negro American all his life—danger of small and great indignities, and of actual physical harm or outright destruction—is something that cannot be conveyed to those who have not lived through it, any more than the feelings and sensations of being in combat can be shared with those to whom it did not happen. These two gulfs between the experienced and the inexperienced can be closed only by the expedients of not having wars and not segregating minorities. The inability of white Americans—even those who want to—fully to comprehend what life is like for the Negro American is one of the two factors which are basic in the lack of understanding between the races.

The other factor is that the white man's complex civilization inevitably makes him sexually jealous of the Negro. There is no rose without its thorns. The many satisfactions of the white man's nonprimitive civilization—enduring family relationships, multiple achievements, etc.—are maintained only by the limitation of his reproductive drive. This not-fully-expended drive makes it impossible for the white man to view sexual activities calmly and without distortion. Because sex is the one department of his life where the dynamics of his civilization compel him to accept incompletion, he tends to regard the sex drive, not as a blessing and the *sine qua non* of his continued stay upon this planet, but as a burden and a curse.

The white man is attracted to and envious of all primitives. It was not just an accident that Dorothy Lamour's sarong gained such a foothold in the national imagination. But he is most intensely fascinated by and jealous of those people living according to a primitive structure right in the same country with him. Incidentally, a similar mechanism no doubt operates for the Negro American. While he may be, in some cases, less frustrated sexually than the white, his drives to be creative and to master the environment are continually thwarted. Hence, full participation in the white man's civilization probably seems to the Negro more enviable than it really is, and there must be many Negroes who do not realize that the white man's civilization has a price tag on it.

Sex being the white American's Achilles' heel, it is as if, when he looks at the Negro American, he had blinders on. He can see only one thing in the Negro—a talent for silken dalliance which he, the white man, does not have. He does not see that this talent exists in different degrees in individual Negroes, and does not necessarily appertain to all Negroes. He assumes that it exists in the same degree

117

—a very considerable degree—in everyone who is born a Negro. He does not see that it is a part, and only one part, of a pattern which has been imposed on the Negro American to serve an economic purpose. He does not see that along with the Negro's sexual pattern goes a pattern of unremitting danger and menace which accompanies him from the cradle to the grave. He does not see how lonely it is for the Negro in these United States.

All the white man sees is the silken dalliance, and all he feels is how much he is tempted to imitate it. But he dare not imitate it, because his whole civilization is based on a minimal use of the reproductive drive, and the white man is therefore afraid—and quite rightly so—that if he attempted to live out a simple sexual pattern in the middle of a complex civilization, he would bring the whole business down about his ears. In this situation, the Caucasian American says, "Get thee behind me, Satan." Through discrimination and segregation, he tries to put the Negro and the whole temptation the Negro stands for as far away from him as possible. That this mechanism also happens to be magnificently convenient for those people who stand to gain, by the maintenance of a permanent low-wage group, completes the vicious circle.

The white man's attempt to fence out the Negro is easily understandable as an instinctive effort to bypass a temptation; but as a practical measure, it is in the same class with throwing yourself under a train in order to cut off a corn. Ironically enough, segregation and discrimination defeat their own end, and only intensify and aggravate the very situation they were designed to minimize. In the first place, it is primitivity in the Negro which disturbs the white man, and fencing off the Negro perpetuates the primitivity and hence guarantees that he will continue to be disturbing. In the second place, every time you erect a barrier against something, you remind yourself, by the very act of putting up the barrier, of what is behind it. There is only one possible way in which the Negro can be made harmless and undisturbing to the white man, and that is not by putting up barriers, but by taking them down.

It is just as true of the Negro as it is of anyone else that he cannot have his cake and eat it, too. If he is free to live wherever he can afford it, to eat wherever he can pay the check, to go to the same schools and churches white people go to, to hold whatever jobs his abilities warrant, he will have to satisfy these ambitions and attain these multiple objectives in the same way the white man does—i.e., at the expense of the reproductive drive. No resolution of the race situation is possible which does not involve remaking the Negro so that he is no longer a symbol of temptation to the white man. The further the Negro gets into complex white society, and the more of its advantages he enjoys, the more also he comes

119

within range of its powerful and chastening disciplines. What the situation calls for is a reversal of the old maxim of divide and conquer. What the situation calls for is to unite and conquer.

IX

"Would You Like Your Daughter to Marry One?"

———

PEOPLE OF good will, and especially people of good will who have daughters, are made very unhappy by the stereotyped old question, "Would you like your daughter to marry one?" They do not wish to say no, because they feel it is a slur on a group of their fellow citizens. On the other hand, they have a dismaying mental picture of the daughter living in Harlem, bearing "coal-black" babies, cut off from family and friends, possibly being ill-treated by the Negro community, and in general leading the life of a miserable outcast. Considering the picture he has in mind, a parent's anxiety is understandable. But he exaggerates the danger. The most persistent mistake the white man makes in his relationship with the Negro is to assume that because he, the Caucasian, has something in mind, the Negro has it in mind, too—which does not necessarily follow.

In his book, *An American Dilemma,* the Swedish scientist, Gunnar Myrdal, compiles a list of what the Negro American wants and another list of what white Americans think the Negro wants. On the Negro's list, intermarriage is at the very bottom. On the white's list, it is at the top. But even without Professor Myrdal's helpful statistics, it does not take much cerebration to figure out that white girls do not marry Negroes, even when they get a chance to meet them socially, because Negroes do not ask them. I have spoken before of the preoccupation of white people, even unprejudiced white people, with their own reaction to the Negro, rather than with the Negro's reaction to them. And there are two elements involved in the issue of intermarriage. One is how the Negro looks to us. The other is how we look to the Negro.

On the record, the white American is, to the Negro, the bully, the lyncher, the coward, the hypocrite—the seeker after empty, two-for-a-nickel "superiority" whose chivalric defense of radiant womanhood consists of sending two hundred armed whites against a solitary unarmed Negro. Even when the white is not himself a sadist and an exploiter, he is too lazy and selfish to do anything effective about curbing the white people who have these qualities, and the arguments he employs to excuse his inactivity would be met with raised eyebrows in a home for the feeble-minded. If we take the trouble to get right out of ourselves, and to consider with unfaltering realism how we must look to other people, it becomes apparent that there is nothing about the American white to make the Negro think we are anything to take home and have around the house.

What attracts the Negro about white people is not what we *are*, but what we *have*—our freedom from humiliation and insult, and the scope we have for gratifying our ambitions and our achievement drives. Negroes are not interested in intermarriage for the very sound reason that there is no percentage in it for them. If they marry white people, they do not move into the white community. They must attempt to take their white partners into the Negro community. From the Negro's point of view, intermarriage simply means that he is saddled with a partner whom racial barriers have made an unassimilable stranger and who arrives in the Negro community with, racially speaking, a morally disreputable background.

Despite the fact that Negro-white marriages are rare, and despite the fact that the Negro needs and wants educational and economic equality a good deal more than he needs and wants interracial unions, intermarriage is a focal issue in Negro-white relations in this country. It is a focal issue because the white American, conditioned by the unavoidable exigents of his society, is fascinated and terrified by the Negro as a sexual symbol. And it will remain a focal issue until the operation of the Christian and democratic conscience has drawn the Negro far enough into complex white society to be modified by its disciplinary pressures and hence to lose his symbolic significance for the white.

That the Christian and democratic conscience is not wholly asleep at the switch is evidenced by the increasing prominence of discussions and activities aimed at improving American race relations. The increased noisiness of the white-supremacy boys is in itself a hopeful sign, because it means that they feel their unwholesome tenets being more and more threatened. Formerly, when the supporters of white supremacy felt less sharply challenged, they were much quieter. An example of the working of the national conscience came my way a year and a half ago in the form of a provocative letter written by a lieutenant in a motor-torpedo-boat squadron in the Pacific. The lieutenant was from the deep South, and after describing himself as one of those "who seek democracy in a nation where it is sometimes hard to find," he continued:

> Even I am not sure how far I would go to insure that democracy. I want my colored friend to vote; I want him

to be free from prejudice in the courts; I want him to go to college; I want him to have the best of living conditions; I want him to be paid what he is worth; I want him to be an active and respected member of any union he desires; I want him to know and enjoy the Four Freedoms. I will work and work hard to see that he—or his sons—gets these things, but—I do not want him to live next door to me; I do not want him to be my house guest; and I do not want him to dance with my daughter. How can I reconcile these conflicting desires?

It was a fair question. I spent a long time over my reply, which went, in part, as follows:

You ask me how you can reconcile these conflicting desires. The answer is, Lieutenant—you can't.

It seems to me that you've got to select either democracy or undemocracy, and then you're stuck with it. If you plump for white supremacy, on account of what are to you very vivid sensations anent your daughter's future suitors, then your delicate conscience is going to make your inner life a hell on earth. But I cannot in honesty deny that everything you do to get educational and economic equality for the Negro brings him one step nearer to dancing with your daughter. Not in your lifetime, perhaps—at least, in the South—and possibly not in hers. But ultimately.

I have the profoundest respect for how deeply implanted your feeling is against accepting Negroes as social equals, and I would no more try to tamper with it than I would try to psychoanalyze you. But I am very much aware of the fact that it wasn't *necessary* for you to have that feeling. It isn't natural or instinctive. It was trained into you—as it has been trained into other people, at other times and in other parts of the world, where a readily identifiable section of the population looked to somebody like a dandy outfit for hewing the wood and drawing the water at virtually no cost.

Othello and *Aïda*—in neither of which is the tragedy at all connected with the fact that one of the contracting parties is colored—illustrate how placidly white people in other countries can accept racial equality. White children in this country have no feeling about Negro children, other than the feelings all children have about each other, until it is taught to them.

The civilization around the eastern end of the Mediterranean has been a hodgepodge of black, yellow and white races since time immemorial, and it was from that civilization that the Crusaders brought back the mathematics, astronomy and celestial navigation that Western Europe hadn't yet been able to think up for itself.

If Old Mother Nature had had any objections to a commingling of the races, she would have fixed it some way so that they could not embrace. (At this juncture, one's mind goes careering off on to speculations as to *how* she would have fixed it. But this, though diverting, is unprofitable.)

It is therefore quite possible to conceive of future Americans who have no more feeling about mingling socially with, and marrying, Negroes than they have about cleaning their teeth. With your background and training, it may be awfully hard for you to imagine this, but that doesn't matter, because you won't be there. Except possibly as a piece of insurgent ectoplasm that the future Americans won't see or hear.

As for you yourself, Lieutenant—I can't see any way to reconcile your conflicting desires. But there is a lot of work to be done on race relations in America this side of social equality, and I think—if I judge you rightly from your letter—you will be happier if you do it. You had better stock up on bicarbonate of soda and try not to think of posterity.

Three months later—my correspondent having been somewhat busy in the interval—I received the following reply:

Perhaps without knowing it, you have supplied me the answer to my dilemma. That answer I find in two points made by you. The first is that we are not born with racial prejudices. We are educated to them, perhaps not formally, but certainly effectively. So it is with me. Your second and all-important point is that everything I do in the interest of the Negro brings him closer to dancing with my daughter. You point out that my efforts in their small way will lead to equality, not in my lifetime, but in hers. After about the tenth reading, light broke like a flare in the darkness.

The answer to my problem is in two words: *SO WHAT?*

What right have I to say with whom my daughter shall dance? Certainly I have no right to dictate the likes and dislikes of my *granddaughter!* If the next generation should by a miracle of education grow up to believe in true democracy and accept all men as equals, what is it to me? That is my daughter's business. All I can or should do is to see that she has an open mind and picks up from her lovely mother or myself enough sense to discern between dead right and dead wrong. With this attitude, I can write what I please and fight racial prejudice with an eye to ultimate victory.

The lieutenant is far from being out of the woods. He is still going to have difficult and frightening decisions to make. For the rest of his life, his upbringing and his idealism will be in conflict. But at least he is not groping in the dark. He knows where he is going. If he is handicapped, he is at least aware of being handicapped and can allow for it. He has arrived at a realistic view of the situation and of himself in relation to it.

I have spoken of his being handicapped, but even white people who were not brought up in the deep South cannot be considered as being very much better off than the lieutenant. In view of the forces

at work in the situation, the integration of the
Negro American into American society will, when
it is finally accomplished, be one of the greatest
monuments to the human spirit in all of history.
Such a task is necessarily long, grim and heartbreaking. The nameless medieval workers who, in their
successive generations, built the Cathedral of Chartres must often have wondered dejectedly whether it
was worth it. They must often have argued fiercely
that, in view of how long it was taking, there was no
sense going on.

The Cathedral of Chartres is not symmetrical, and
nothing done by human beings ever comes out exactly even. As intermarriage ultimately develops,
there will probably be a small group of whites who
marry only whites; a small group of Negroes who
marry only Negroes; and a much larger group in between of Negroes and whites who feel free to marry
each other *if they want to*. It is a mistake to try to
envision that future in terms of the way many white
Americans feel now. By the time such an era arrives,
the necessary adjustments to it will have been made.
Many white people now living believe that they are
repelled by the kinky hair of the Negro and feel that
no greater disaster could befall them than to have
children or grandchildren with kinky hair. But it is
perfectly possible to imagine a time when no one
will pay any attention to kinky hair, one way or the
other. The distaste for kinky hair is not inborn. It is

a superficial conditioning, imposed from the outside, and we are not justified in assuming that it will
continue to be imposed forever.

People's ideas change. How much they change can
only be realized by looking back at some of the
things that used to be believed. Women of my age
can remember a time when we bound ourselves
down to look as flat-chested as possible, and wore
dresses like grain sacks with narrow belts right spang
(God save the mark!) around the widest part of our
hips. Those clothes so distorted, maligned and mis-
represented the female figure that when we look at
them now, they seem shocking and almost blasphemous. But once we thought them beautiful. Once
they didn't seem blasphemous at all.

There was a time when sincere and well-meaning
people felt, and felt passionately, that to administer
an anesthetic for an operation was to flout the will
of God. It seems incredible now that human beings
could have formulated a Deity who rejoices in our
pain and who would be angry if we were spared any
of it; but once it seemed not only plausible, but
changeless and eternal. In the same way, the feelings, myths and prejudices about the Negro American which now seem so vivid and real to some of our
white contemporaries will take their place on the
shelf along with the belief in witches and the notion
that the earth is the center of the solar system.

X

The Care and Feeding of Bigots

THE GENERAL atmosphere of American civilization is protestant (with a small *p*), self-reliant, and emotionally optimistic; but even the youngest and strongest culture is not without its morbid elements. We have in this country a collection of white people —not all of them Southerners—who are fanatically prejudiced against Negroes. These people constitute a considerable obstacle to improved Negro-white relations. Considerable, but not insuperable. If you examine the mechanics underlying this kind of prejudice, it does not seem entirely hopeless of treatment.

Passionately prejudiced people always turn out,

under scrutiny, to be people who cannot get along on a footing of equality with anyone, either Negro or white. We once had a brilliant example of this at the canteen in the person of a hard-bitten matron who called the Negro servicemen "niggers" and tried to segregate them from the Caucasians, but who had hysterics every time we asked her to leave. It turned out, upon investigation, that the lady was a desperate and incurable social climber and celebrity chaser and she thought the canteen, which enjoyed a considerable prestige, would be a place where she could meet luminaries.

About the whole setup, there was a kind of infelicitous bookkeeping. The snubs the matron administered to the Negroes, she in turn received from the brilliant and successful people who correctly assayed her thinness of character and could not be bothered with her. This woman could not learn to adopt a democratic attitude toward the Negro servicemen who came to the canteen because she had never been in a democratic situation in her whole life.

A conspicuous instance of people who must always be either inferiors or superiors are those Southerners who oppress and exploit the Negro and at the same time put "Southern womanhood" on a fluted pedestal, before which they prostrate themselves in postures of unbecoming abjection. But other examples of the same behavior pattern abound: men who are inordinately scornful of Jews, Negroes, Catholics, foreigners, or other minorities, but who occupy year after endless year a position of marital inferiority to a dominating wife. Or women who are callous, condescending and heartless with all their beaux except one, and with that one occupy a position of crawling and whimpering inferiority.

The only people capable of equality, with anyone, are people *who are themselves used to being treated as equals.* Stubborn, unyielding prejudice is always—and this is axiomatic—an attempt to restore a balance. An individual finds himself in an inferior relationship to somebody or something. It may be wife, husband, parent, or employer. It may be, as in the case of the Southern poor whites, a cruel and oppressive economic situation. But if the individual believes his position to be hopeless, he instinctively tries to match the inferior-superior situation in which he is the inferior with another inferior-superior situation in which he is the superior.

A seemingly ineradicable belief in the "inferiority" of the Negro is not a simple, single item that exists by itself. It is a response to a stimulus. It is a thing which comes after something that has already gone before. And the key to such prejudice is hopelessness. A person who finds himself the underdog, but who has reason to believe he can get out of the situation, is not implacably prejudiced. It is the people who have given up hope of ever getting out from under who hate and despise minorities. In trying to change such people, the attack has to be mainly on the oppressive force (whatever it is) which created the prejudice, rather than on the prejudice itself.

There is another set of people who constitute an obstacle to improved Negro-white relations. These are the people who are unprejudiced, but who have a sort of fashionable despair about the race situation. They do not do anything about it because they feel it is so hopeless there is no use trying. Less morbid than the violently prejudiced, these people probably do just as much damage to the emotional atmosphere in which we are facing the problem as the fanatical Negrophobes.

An apparent meaning is given to this fashionable despair by the clamor of persons like Representative Rankin and his unpolished followers. But it is only an apparent meaning. Naturally, but misleadingly, unsuccessful race relations always get into the papers, whereas successful ones, being undramatic, do not so often find their way into the public prints.* Wildly intolerant people catch the public eye more often than completely tolerant ones—possibly because intolerant people are innately more exhibitionistic. If

* The canteen where I worked was one of the most well-known organizations of its kind in the country. But the one thing that really distinguished it from other canteens—its successful maintenance of an interracial policy—was almost never mentioned in the voluminous public notices it received.

the strongly prejudiced people in this country had as much of a following as one would think, from the racket they make, American race relations would already have collapsed into anarchy.

Hopelessness about the race situation is an attitude which needs to be examined carefully. It sometimes turns out to be a concealed form of arrogance. One grim story in an upper-crust magazine does not prove that Negro-white relations are irretrievably ruined. One unpleasing incident witnessed in a bus is not conclusive. That the story is written and published, that the incident is regarded as shocking, shows that the national conscience is still doing business at the old stand. Our knowledge, as Saint Paul said, is piecemeal. Only a person informed about every major and minor event in race relations all over the country would be in a position to say whether or not the future is hopeless. The fact is that nobody knows as yet whether it is hopeless. All we know is that it can be made hopeless, if enough people choose to consider it so.

This fashionable despair is not usually the product of a prolonged and careful study of American race relations. It is usually the product of a maladjustment between the despairing individual and the culture in which he lives. Any given person takes things out of the culture every day and all day long. The medicines that keep him alive, the ideas that absorb him, the pretty girls he looks at, the solace of religion—all these and a thousand other things he accepts from his civilization. If, in return, he puts nothing back in, it follows as the night the day that he will be nervous and ill at ease. There has to be mutuality between the individual and his civilization, or else the individual feels lonely, frightened and overwhelmed. He has an oppressive sense that the culture forms him, but no corresponding realization that he forms the culture. Because he is not taking his own part in shaping and controlling the culture, he assumes that it is uncontrollable and that no climax can be anticipated except disaster.

It must be admitted that a certain amount of sincere, and apparently justifiable despair is produced by the appearance in our national scene of such persons as Senator Bilbo. But while the Senator is undeniably a gaudy specimen, he is somewhat less ominous than he would like us to think. A situation like that of the Negro in our society inevitably produces people who are eloquent about it, on either side. It produces Lillian Smiths, John Browns, John C. Calhouns, Harriet Beecher Stowes, John Rankins, William Lloyd Garrisons, Richard Wrights, William Dudley Pelleys. It produces Senator Bilbo and it produces Abraham Lincoln. The Senator is only one of a long line of people who have been thrust to the surface by the dynamics of the race situation.

Senator Bilbo operates on the familiar, small-boy principle that it is better to be considered a blot on the landscape than not to be noticed at all. There are few adults, however seasoned, who cannot on occasion be hoaxed by a really determined small boy. And the Senator takes us over the bumps, there is no denying that. He gets us to play his game. Newspapers and pulpits and living rooms all over the country ring with horrified exclamations after each of his outrageous performances. But when the smoke of participles clears away, the Negro-white setup remains as it was. Which is just what the Senator intended. He wins on two counts. He gets our attention, which is obviously pleasing to him, and he diverts our energy into verbal rather than practical channels.

We have little time for the Senator. We have too much to do. He has only one idea, and he has already said it. Had we any leisure, we might spare him a little pity, for he has the symptoms of a man being driven nearly crazy by a complete absence of self-respect. People cannot live without self-respect. If they cannot come by it honestly, they will get it (or some substitute for it) dishonestly; but come hell or high water, they will get it. They have to, in order to stay alive. There are thirteen million Negroes in this country; five million Jews; twenty-four million Catholics; and eleven and a half million foreign-born. The Senator's desperate inner hollowness can be measured by the fact that it requires fifty-three and a half million people, highhandedly classified as his inferiors, to prop him up enough so that he can get up and eat his breakfast and get to work in the morning.

The point will immediately be made that Hitler, too, was pitiable and laughable. Admittedly, there is a parallel. The Senator uses Hitler's formula of taking an extremely simple idea and saying it over and over. But the parallel breaks off here: democracy produces *both* heroes and villains, but it differs from a fascist state in that it does not produce a hero who *is* a villain. The point is not whether Bilbo is like Hitler, but whether we are like the Germans—passive, sheeplike and very, very easily bluffed.

There are forty-eight states in this Union, and the citizens of forty-seven of them do not have to take the responsibility of having elected Theodore Bilbo to the Senate. Nor can anything be inferred about the future of America merely from conditions in the single commonwealth of Mississippi. The citizens of the other forty-seven states can do a great deal of work, both major and minor, to make America American without encountering any effective interference from the gentleman from Mississippi.

Senator Bilbo blankets the whole topic of race relations with such a mantle of exhibitionistic vulgarity that he makes the entire subject seem like a vaudeville act in purgatory. But this is only an illusion which, astutely and cleverly, he creates. He creates it for the purpose, in which he often succeeds, of paralyzing the millions and millions of decent, fair-minded Americans who have both the wish and the power to relax racial tensions. The key to the Senator is this: he does not deal *with* problems. He trades *on* them. The hope of the race situation lies in that very numerous body of Americans who are accustomed to dealing *with* problems because that is the way they spend their lives.

XI

The Solid South and the Frozen North

———

WHITE PEOPLE, discussing race relations, spend a great deal of time talking about the nature of the Negro. The Negro is (or is not) a child; the Negro is (or is not) lazy; etc., etc. But the nature of the Negro is more or less irrelevant. Any group of people subjected to a consistent course of treatment, good or bad, will bear the earmarks of that treatment. If you change the treatment, the earmarks change, too. The fact to be recognized is not the nature of the Negro, but the nature of democracy. It is the nature of democracy that you cannot discriminate against a minority, inside a democratic framework, without creating the bitterest resentment in that minority.

In a totalitarian regime, openly rejoicing in concentration camps and secret police, it may be possible arbitrarily to stigmatize a section of the populace and have them accept it passively and without much wish to retaliate. In such a country, a heavy propaganda machine works all the time at reducing the will to resist. But in a democracy—where there is no official fascist propaganda machine, and where the signs and symbols and slogans all have to do with liberty and equality—a segregated minority is going to hate its segregators just as sure as God made little apples. This is not Negro nature, but human nature, which resents false promises a good deal more intensively than it resents no promises at all.

To forget for a single moment the steady, pulsing tide of Negro resentment is to lose one of the main threads in the tangled skein of interracial relationships. Much Negro conduct is partially explainable in terms of this resentment, and some of it is explainable only in such terms. In those parts of the South where there are large communities of uneducated and untrained Negroes, a popular argument against racial equality is that the Negro is an unreliable employee and only comes to work when he feels like it. This behavior is brought forward as evidence of an irresponsibility which (it is said) unfits the Negro for the role of first-class citizen.

But that is only one possible interpretation. You can make the Negro ride in Jim Crow cars. You can

141

deny him the right to vote, neglect his schooling, and shut him out of all the challenging and stimulating jobs. You can even, if life seems unbearably dull, select a Negro more or less at random and lynch him. But there is one thing you cannot do. You cannot make him work if he doesn't want to. His refusal to take work seriously—in those cases where he does refuse to take it seriously—may very well be his way of striking back. It may be that, having observed how much importance white people attach to getting things done, he hits them where he knows it will hurt by laughing at work and denying its value.

The important thing about human beings is not what they do, but why they do it. Some people I know, seeing a Negro Army captain sitting alone in a hotel lounge, invited him to join them in a drink. He did, and my friends were puzzled and hurt to find that the captain's angry bitterness toward white people seemed to extend even to them, although they are by nature spontaneously friendly. Some white people react to all Negroes as The Negro. With equal blindness, some Negroes react to all white people as The White. To be snubbed for a sincere and well-meant gesture is not enjoyable, but the rebuff does not necessarily have to be accepted as personal. The Negro in question may not be seeing *you*. He may be seeing the Negro troops who broke through a steaming Pacific jungle and found a "For White Only" sign on the sole available water truck.

Negro resentment is sometimes misplaced and sometimes shrill, hysterical and tasteless. But no matter what form it takes—and on occasion it has overpowering dignity—the Negro's resentment is a good omen. It shows how pervasive democracy is. It shows that the idea of democracy has penetrated into every layer and stratum of our society, in spite of those who wish otherwise. In addition, the resentment of our Negro compatriots is a testimonial to their inner vitality and quickness of spirit and, as such, it bodes well for the future and we would do well to rejoice in it.

Southerners are usually much more frightened by Negro resentment than Northerners, who tend to be much less aware of it. Among my souvenirs are a number of letters from Southerners who say that I and other Northerners who have not lived or traveled in the South have no right to "interfere" in the relations between Negroes and whites in this country. For different reasons, both Northerners and Southerners often make the mistake of assuming that the race situation is an exclusively Southern problem. Actually, it is an American problem. While it has different aspects in the North and in the South, anything that is done about it, good or bad, has national repercussions; and the individual citizen is involved, not as a Northerner or as a Southerner, but as an American.

If the race situation is anybody's special and exclusive problem, it is almost truer to say that it is the North's rather than the South's. The North has a greater responsibility than the South because it has the superior equipment for dealing with the problem. The North has a more bracing climate than many parts of the South. It is a richer section of the country, with all that that implies in terms of general levels of health and education. And while many Northern citizens are prejudiced against Negroes, that prejudice is not usually trained into them so intensively or at so early an age as is customary in the South.

When I first worked at the canteen, I was shocked to the marrow at the attitude of some of the Southern servicemen toward our Negro compatriots, and I said so with considerable heat. But after a while I began to realize that these denunciations, though affording me considerable personal satisfaction, were not perceptibly improving the lot of the Negro American. My feeling has since come to be that, from a common-sense standpoint, denouncing the South is like saying to someone with appendicitis, "Brother, you had no business having an inflamed appendix in the first place. But since you've been stupid enough to get one, just go tear it out with your bare hands and don't expect any help from me." The Northerner, offended and angered by Southern sentiments, has only one telling and effective answer: that is, to take a personal interest in and responsibility for letting down racial barriers in the North, where it is somewhat easier to do.

To permit our Negro minority to spread out is the paramount necessity of the race situation, and the first steps in this direction will have to be taken by the people best fitted to do it—i.e., the Northerners. The circular dilemma into which white people fall is to herd Negroes into ghettos, because they are afraid of them, and then to be afraid of them because they never see them except in phalanxes. But white Americans outnumber Negro Americans ten to one, and the area of the United States is three million square miles. Speaking geographically, there is plenty of room for our Negro minority to fan out and virtually disappear in the crowd.

Most white people are acquainted with Negroes only in menial capacities, and this, with rare exceptions, is the only sort of Negro ever portrayed in the movies or over the radio. To the average white person, therefore, social equality suggests compulsory association with the only kind of Negro he has ever seen—the Negro in the humble job. In reality, there are fifty-five thousand Negro college graduates in this country, as well as a flourishing, respectable Negro middle class. But few white people know anything about them, because they are not permitted to live or work in the places where their cultural and commercial interests would naturally lead them, if they were not Negroes.

Northerners find it hard to remember, though most of them know, that a basic reason for the violence of Southern attitudes is the larger proportion of the Negro minority which lives in the South. If Northerners opened up jobs and schools and churches and neighborhoods to Negroes—not just in the big Northern industrial centers, but particularly in the smaller Northern population units—some of the South's overlarge proportion of Negro residents would be drained away from it. In this way, the tension of Southern whites would be somewhat diminished. They would feel less threatened by the "black tide" of which they have a genuine, if unrealistic, terror, and the way would be clearer than it is now for Southern liberals to work toward racial equality in the South. Last, but by no means least, it would be much more difficult to use the Negroes as cheap labor if they were encouraged to leave their sealed-in communities (wherever they exist) and to distribute themselves more evenly through the various ranks and strata of the white population. A beginning would then be made in breaking up the vicious circle of sexual fear of the Negro and manipulation of that fear by interested parties to keep him as an exploited worker.

The dubious reader—and surely I have a dubious reader?—is going to point out that this sounds fine on paper, but neither Negro Americans nor white Americans are ready for it. Which is quite true.

They are not. A large proportion of our Negro minority has not had the schooling to equip it for more challenging jobs or more responsible situations than it has now. A proportion—to date, we do not know how small or large—of our white majority has not yet outgrown its blustering, childish self-love. But life, unfortunately, does not wait until people are ready for things. The families whose sons were killed in the war were not ready to be bereaved. The tides of history do not pause at the flood and slap about aimlessly, awaiting our convenience. History, in the old phrase of hide-and-seek, says, ". . . eight, nine, *ten.* Ready or not, I'm COMing!"

To avoid crippling disillusionments, steps taken to improve race relations have to be made in the full knowledge that some Negro Americans and some white Americans are not ready for them. At the same time that we open jobs to Negroes that have not been held by Negroes before, and neighborhoods to Negroes where they have not lived before, we will have to be providing the education which will make them equal to their new responsibilities. Simultaneously, we will have to educate white people the way the canteen educated them—by laboratory demonstrations that interracial projects will not only work, but will free the white people who participate in them of a very considerable burden of guilt.

We will, to sum up, have to do many things at once. This is neither so novel nor so frightening a prospect as may at first be imagined. Any woman who keeps house can testify that the moment the doorbell rings is almost always the precise, identical segment of time when the rice boils over and the baby falls downstairs. There is nothing especially new to human experience in having to take care of everything at once. Wives and mothers and Henry J. Kaiser do it all the time. It is often, as a matter of fact, referred to with pride as The American Tradition. "The difficult we do right away. The impossible takes a little bit longer."

XII

"Little Drops of Water, Little Grains of Sand"

―――

W HEN THE canteen's no-discrimination policy was
described to them, people sometimes used to
say, "Yes, that's all very well, but you haven't produced a solution." And they were quite right. The
canteen did not produce a "solution" to the race
problem because there isn't any "solution" to it, any
more than there is a "solution" to marriage. Only in
fairy tales do people live happily ever after. There is
no perfect way of living with our Negro compatriots,
any more than there is a perfect way of living with
one's husband or wife. But there are better ways
right at our finger tips than we are using now.

What are they?

What can any given individual do?

What you can do depends on where you live and the circumstances of your life. But where there's a will, there's a way.

The main thing is to select something that is in line with your own personality and something that falls within the framework of your life as that framework is already set up. Some people are naturally efficient, manipulatory and not afraid of obstacles. Others, while daunted by obstacles, have tact and the blessed ability to pour oil on troubled waters. Some people with brilliantly constructive ideas have no staying power; while others, though less imaginative, are quietly tenacious. Whatever your particular virtue, there is need for it.

No matter what your temperament or circumstances, you can write letters to radio stations, newspapers, institutions and individuals—Congressmen, for instance—applauding them when they take a courageous stand about race relations or expressing disapproval when they are backward and regressive. Public institutions and public figures are notoriously timid. Letters, in sufficient quantities, have often proved a powerful weapon. Such letters need not be either long or eloquent. All you have to do is make clear which side you are on.

You can give money, if you have it, to organizations that are working for improved race relations. The National Association for the Advancement of Colored People (20 West 40th Street, New York), the National Urban League (1133 Broadway, New York), the Southern Regional Council (63 Auburn Avenue, Atlanta, Georgia), and the Southern Conference on Human Welfare (212½ Union Street, Nashville 3, Tennessee), are the four most outstanding. The first two are national in scope. The two last named operate only in the South. Other organizations, though not devoted exclusively to racial democracy, include it as part of their program. The Federal Council of Churches and the Y.W.C.A. have both avowed as one of their objectives the end of segregation and discrimination. If you are on the alert for news about race relations, you will read or hear about still other groups, some national and some local, which work in whole or in part for racial democracy.

And you can always read. Lillian Smith's *Strange Fruit* and/or Richard Wright's *Native Son* and *Black Boy* you may already be familiar with. There is, in addition, an enormous literature on the subject, and any librarian in a public or rental library can make suggestions. The definitive book on race relations in America is Gunnar Myrdal's *An American Dilemma,* but this is over a thousand pages long and the average citizen, with a job to hold down or a home to run, probably does not have time to get through all of it. However, if you can borrow it from the library, or from someone who owns a copy, you can read parts of it—selecting from its lucid table of contents the chapters that look to you most interesting.

If you live near a library which has them, you might glance at the Negro newspapers and magazines. They may startle you—Myrdal describes the Negro press as a fighting press, and strongly opinionated—but they will give you increased awareness of minority heartaches. The *Negro Digest* and the picture magazine *Ebony* will interest the general reader most. *Crisis* is the organ of the N.A.A.C.P. and *Opportunity* of the National Urban League. As for newspapers, the Norfolk *Journal and Guide,* the Baltimore *Afro-American,* the Pittsburgh *Courier,* the Chicago *Defender,* the New York *Age,* and New York's *Amsterdam News* and *People's Voice* vary in attitudes, but are alike in being written for Negro readers at various cultural levels.

A list of books on race relations is attached to the end of this chapter. It is very, very far from being inclusive, but it will do for a start.

If you belong to a businessman's club or a literary or discussion group, you can get together with some of the other members and suggest to the program committee that a Negro speaker be invited to lecture. He need not necessarily lecture on race relations. He can speak on whatever subject happens to be his particular field. If you are a church member, you can round up some of the other parishioners who see eye to eye with you and broach the subject of inviting a Negro minister to fill the pulpit on some appropriate occasion.

Reading, writing letters, giving money, having discussion groups, and securing Negro speakers and artists are about all you can do, if you live in a community which has no Negro residents. In such a community, you and your friends and neighbors can only prepare yourselves and wait upon circumstance. But this preparation is a clear duty. Communities with no Negro residents—even though it is no fault of their own—have to be carried by the communities with too many Negro residents. When some white people have no immediate responsibility, it means that other white people have a double load—white people in Detroit, New York, Chicago, some of the West Coast cities, and, of course, the whole South.

In our fast-moving world, it is impossible to tell when a person or a community may be called upon to be maturely democratic. In a small Eastern city, about a year ago, a Negro doctor moved into a white residential neighborhood. Consternation ensued. The local peasantry scattered garbage on the doctor's front walk. The more aristocratic element formed a committee, called on the newcomer, and offered to buy his house for a great deal of money. As a matter of principle, the doctor declined. He continued to occupy his house, keeping it neat and living unobtrusively. Within a year, he had demonstrated his respectability to a point where he was invited to join the country club. Happily, the people in this neighborhood were intelligent enough to learn from actual experience. But had they been educated beforehand, they could have spared themselves a trying emotional ordeal.

Incidentally, although they learned to get on pleasantly with the doctor, they did not want any more Negro residents. Or, at least, not very many. And their reaction was a sensible one. Merely to move the Negro ghettos from one place to another accomplishes nothing. Where the race situation is concerned, conscientious communities cannot take over the responsibilities of lackadaisical ones, even if they want to. It is a problem that, like a mosaic, can be worked out only by a great many small contributions. No heroes need apply.

If you live in a community which has Negro residents, it is easier to find things to do. Perhaps your children go to schools or camps or belong to clubs which exclude Negro children or merely do not happen to have any. Perhaps you and the other parents can arrange for the admission of a few Negro children. It should be more than one, because that places too much of a burden on the Negro child, but it should not be too many. The idea is for the school to absorb them, not for them to absorb the school. Working with children is the easiest part of educating for democracy, because children are still undefeated and have no stake in being prejudiced.

Where it is at all possible for the school or camp to select some of its teachers or counselors from among qualified Negroes, this is even more desirable. Example is better than precept. Children are naturally imitative and are much influenced by the behavior of adults. When they see adults of both races working together on a common job, it impresses them at deeper levels of their minds than lectures, or even than the companionship of Negro children.

If you are an employer, it may be possible for you to make a point of hiring a Negro or Negroes, if qualified ones are available. "How are you going to make Negro and white employees work together?" is a favorite query of employers. By employers with prestige and qualities of leadership, it can be done. In essence, the problem is one of public relations, and public relations is supposed to be the *specialité de la maison* of American business.

A community with Negro residents may very well have public or private organizations devoted to Negro welfare in one way or another. You can get into contact with these groups. If you don't know their names, write to your mayor or Chamber of Commerce, or ask your minister or one of your civic leaders. Even if such organizations are limited or inept in their functions, you can find out through them what the general setup is and who are the leaders of the Negro community. These bodies may, on the other hand, be functioning extremely well, but they will still be glad of your interest and support. They can use it. If you find these organizations unsatisfactory, perhaps you and your friends can breathe new life into them. If no such groups exist in your community, you can create them.

Such organizations should be interracial and should be constructed so that Negroes and whites work together on problems that concern the community *as a whole*. Guilty benevolence—tossing the Negroes a housing project so that you will go to heaven when you die—does no good and may even do harm. You cannot atone for the sins of other white people, living or dead, and it is silly to try. The righteous resentment of the Negro American is a fact that has to be allowed for and dealt with, just as the presence of thirty-six inches in a yard is a fact that has to be allowed for and dealt with; but nothing is gained by getting sentimental about it. So far as white people are concerned, there is one simple rule for interracial projects: don't try to atone for the past. Forget about the past and build for the future.

Here are a few notes that may be helpful:

1. Don't overdo. When you start in to work for improved race relations, pick some goal that you have a reasonable chance of achieving. The integration of the Negro into American society is a job for the long pull. It is foolish to knock yourself out right in the beginning.

2. Don't be surprised when you find jealousy, back-biting, rivalry and pettiness among your Negro compatriots. These qualities exist among Negroes in about the same degree that they exist among Caucasians.

3. Don't expect to find that all Negroes think alike and agree among themselves as to the best means for their advancement. White people do not think uniformly and in a mass, and neither do Negroes. There are great differences of opinion among Negroes as to what are the most judicious courses for them to pursue, and these differences are sometimes argued hotly.

4. When you first start meeting and working with your Negro fellow citizens, you will probably feel both noble and nervous, in about equal parts. This is uncomfortable, but it wears off.

5. Be prepared to recognize overstrain among your Negro friends or coworkers, if evidences of it should appear. In an excellent pamphlet called *There Are Things to Do,* reprinted from the Winter 1942–43 number of *South Today,* Lillian Smith says:

   The Negro race is a sane, stable race of people who have under trying conditions proved themselves strong and creative and wise; but they are at present subjected to as severe psychic strain as a people ever had to endure on the face of the earth. Their nerves give way, as do ours; their frustrations reach the place where self-control is not always the master. They get to the point where they just can't take any more.

Don't, however, adopt a Florence Nightingale or Nurse's Aide attitude toward all Negroes. Some Negroes are extremely well balanced and well integrated and show fewer signs of strain than you do.

6. Sooner or later, in every interracial venture, the issue comes up of the Negro who has been rejected for some position or other, because he is not qualified, and who then makes the welkin ring with cries that he has been discriminated against solely for reasons of color. Just as some white people are guiltily benevolent toward the Negro, so some Negroes try to trade on the white man's sense of guilt.

If, in these cases, it is possible to train or educate or condition the Negro so that he will be suitable for whatever the position is, that should be done. But if there is no way of making him the right person for the place, it is better to stick to your guns, even though the outcry is likely to be terrific. Intelligent and responsible Negroes will respect you for maintaining standards and not letting yourself be bullied into what, after all, only amounts to empty and unconstructive charity.

7. Don't force equality on Negroes who are fright-

ened by it. Sometimes elderly Negroes, or Negroes just up from the deep South, are more alarmed than gratified by gestures of equality. In these cases, don't press the matter. You have fulfilled your obligation by offering equality. If the Negro is too apprehensive to accept it, that is his business. The main job is to see that young Negroes now growing up are not conditioned to be afraid of white people.

In any enterprise, large or small, which is designed to make Negro and white Americans less self-conscious with each other, the most important thing to hang on to is a sense of perspective. In spite of the perils through which our country has passed, or seemed to pass, we are still here. We are still here, and we are still functioning as an official democracy. We are not functioning brilliantly as a democracy, but we never have. Brilliance is not an attribute of democracies—which, when they cease to bumble and fumble and lurch and sprawl toward their goals, also cease to be democracies.

When our form of government is actually *on* the scrap heap, we will have the rest of eternity to sit around mourning it in our most fluting cadences. In the meantime, fashionable melancholy and immobilizing despair need to be looked at sharply. They may be sincere, but on the other hand, they sometimes serve as an excuse for idleness and a screen for irresponsibility—for taking everything out of the culture and putting nothing back in. With one indisputable fact we may comfort ourselves. Our Negro compatriots are not committing suicide in droves. They are not going around shooting white Americans at random, on the ground that they have nothing to lose. They, at least, still have a little faith in us.

The integration of the Negro into American society is one of the most exciting challenges to self-development and self-mastery that any nation of people ever faced. Obviously such a task will continue to be punctuated—as it is punctuated now—with disillusionment, violence and terror. Many people fear that an epidemic of race riots is on the horizon. If such riots materialize, it is important to remember that, shocking and sickening as they are, they do not necessarily spell finis. We can surmount them. We can even build on them, if we make a conscious effort to channelize the moral indignation they evoke into positive and practical measures for a more comfortable democracy.

The principal thing to keep in mind is this: the disillusionment, violence and terror do not exist just by themselves. They have a clear and unmistakable relationship to the magnitude of the task and the magnificence of the stakes. "Out of this nettle, danger, we pluck this flower, safety."

A Short List of Suggested Reading

Brothers Under the Skin, by Carey McWilliams. Mr. McWilliams is a well-known writer on the subject of prejudice.

W. E. B. Du Bois' autobiography, *Dusk of Dawn.*

George Washington Carver, by Rackham Holt, if you haven't already read it.

Brown Americans and *Thirteen Against the Odds,* by Edwin Embree. These are both informative and not difficult reading.

A Primer for White Folks. This is an anthology of pieces by both white and Negro writers, compiled by Bucklin Moon.

The Darker Brother, a novel by Bucklin Moon.

A Rising Wind, by Walter White—a study of discrimination in the armed forces during the war.

Race Riot, by Alfred McClung Lee, and *To Stem This Tide,* by Charles S. Johnson, are both about the prevention of race riots and about measures for lessening racial tensions.

New World A-Comin', by Roi Ottley, is about the Negro in New York City, and *Black Metropolis,* by Horace Cayton and St. Clair Drake, is about the Negro in Chicago.

All American, by John R. Tunis, is a book for young people on the subject of race prejudice.

What the Negro Wants, edited by Rayford W. Logan. The introduction to this, by one W. C. Couch, has been much criticized, but the main body consists of articles by fourteen outstanding Negro Americans.

Race: Science and Politics, by Ruth Benedict.

Race and Rumors of Race, by Howard Odum. Mr. Odum is president of the Southern Regional Council and a prominent white Southern liberal.

Characteristics of the American Negro, by Otto E. Klineberg.

The Negro Family in the United States, by E. Franklin Frazier.

The Negro's Share, by Richard Sterner, who, like Gunnar Myrdal, is a Swedish scientist.

The Story of the Springfield Plan, by Clarence I. Chatto.

Build Together, Americans and *Get Together, Americans,* by Rachel Du Bois.

Mrs. Palmer's Honey, by Fannie Cook, is a novel about middle-class Negroes in St. Louis. Pleasant reading.

Freedom Road, by Howard Fast, you may already have read. It is a novel about a Negro community in the South right after the Civil War, and it enjoyed a considerable success.

The Negro in Art, by Alain Locke.

They Seek a City, by Arna Bontemps and Jack Conroy, is about Negro migration.

The Street, by Ann Petry. This novel is an instructive study of the relentless and brutalizing pressures which mold lower-income-group Negroes in the packed and stifling ghetto of Harlem.

Hortense Powdermaker's *Probing Our Prejudices* is a well-known book on the subject.

All Brave Sailors, by John Beecher, is about the S.S. *Booker T. Washington.*

African Journey is by Eslanda Robeson, Paul Robeson's wife.

Deep River, by Henrietta Buckmaster, has a continuing reputation. It is a novel about the minority in the Georgia legislature which voted against secession.

Color and Conscience by Buell G. Gallagher, a study, by a churchman, of race prejudice in terms of Christianity.

Sense and Nonsense About Race by Ethel J. Alpenfels, a very readable little pamphlet by an anthropologist.

A NOTE ABOUT THE AUTHOR

———

IT WASN'T *until she went to England for a year in 1936–1937 that Margaret Halsey discovered that all was grist that came to her mill. She thereupon sat down and wrote a book called* With Malice Toward Some. *It sold a mere matter of some 600,000 copies.*

Prior to that delightful auctorial experience, Miss Halsey was born in Yonkers, New York. She got her B.S. from Skidmore College, her M.A. from Teachers College, and then worked—in moderately rapid succession—for a bank, a real estate company, a radio agent, and a publisher. Then came that trip to England.

After Pearl Harbor, she volunteered for work in a

canteen. Her experiences prompted the writing of another best-selling book, this time a novel: Some of My Best Friends Are Soldiers.

For a number of years Miss Halsey has been troubled, as have so many other Americans, by the absence of democracy in Negro-white relationships. The no-discrimination policy of the canteen where she worked gave her answers that she felt she should pass along to others. Color Blind—*a solution book and not a "problem" book—is the result.*